LONDON'S TRULY STRANGEST TALES

Other titles in the STRANGEST series

Cricket's Strangest Matches
Cycling's Strangest Tales
Fishing's Strangest Tales
Football's Strangest Matches
Golf's Strangest Rounds
Horse Racing's Strangest Tales
Kent's Strangest Tales
Law's Strangest Cases
London's Strangest Tales
Medicine's Strangest Cases
Motor Racing's Strangest Races
Rugby's Strangest Matches
Running's Strangest Tales
Shakespeare's Strangest Tales
Teachers' Strangest Tales
Tennis's Strangest Matches

Titles coming soon

Railway's Strangest Tales
Royalty's Strangest Tales

LONDON'S TRULY STRANGEST TALES

Extraordinary but true stories
from almost 2,000 years of London's history

TOM QUINN

PORTICO

ACKNOWLEDGEMENTS

Thanks to all those who pointed me in the direction of strange and quirky stories about London, but especially to the ever-helpful staff of the British Library rare books department.

First published in the United Kingdom in 2017 by
Portico
43 Great Ormond Street
London
WC1N 3HZ

An imprint of Pavilion Books Company Ltd

ISBN 978-1-91104-244-0

A CIP catalogue record for this book is available from the British Library.

10 9 8 7 6 5 4 3 2 1

Reproduction by Mission Productions Ltd, Hong Kong
Printed and bound by Bookwell, Finland

This book can be ordered direct from the publisher at www.pavilionbooks.com

CONTENTS

*And marbled clouds go scudding by
The many-steepled London sky.*

(*John Betjeman,* Selected Poems)

INTRODUCTION

The success of the original *London's Strangest Tales*, which was published more than ten years ago, prompted me to wander ever further along the byways of London's history to discover more remarkable, odd, quirky and often bizarre stories.

This book contains the very best of these stories, which represent years of research in obscure, long-forgotten newspapers and books. London has such a fascinating and complex history that it is hardly surprising there are so many stories still to be told, but even I was amazed at the masses of wonderful material I was able to unearth second time around, as it were.

Here you will find stories of ghosts and eccentrics, mad vicars and dotty aristocrats, who all left their mark on what might best be called an alternative history of the capital.

In addition to these stories, there are strange tales about the built environment and the physical landscape of London; its parks and rivers, graveyards, houses, churches and offices.

Of course, as buildings have been altered, refurbished or demolished over the centuries the whole landscape of the capital has changed, but Londoners are inherently conservative and often, for no apparent reason (other, perhaps, than sentimentality), they like to ensure that parts of ancient and significant buildings are left hidden in odd corners long after the main buildings have changed use or been pulled down. Sometimes sections of old buildings are incorporated into new buildings or preserved in basements or attics. If you want to find these strange and surprising survivors then this is the book for you.

Much of *London's Truly Strangest Tales* concerns itself with the old City, the famous square mile, but there are also stories from the distant suburbs and from south of the river – London over the water, as it has long been known.

Perhaps best of all, *London's Truly Strangest Tales* gives you both an unusual history of one of the world's great cities as well as a guide to some of its least-known and most unusual surviving treasures.

ROMAN SPRING

C.75AD

Where Queen Victoria Street meets the old Huggin Hill, there is a tiny green space – known as Cleary Gardens – with an old brick wall with stone foundations that seem far older. This peaceful corner has never been built on because it is the site of a Roman bathhouse built some time during the first century AD, and the frigidarium and tepidarium and other rooms remain to be excavated under the nearby houses. Medieval vintners subsequently used the site for trading and growing vines.

Part of the Roman wall can still be seen below the Victorian wall and the spring that once served the bathhouse bubbled forth until fairly recently.

ROMAN REMAINS

C.300AD

There are very few obvious Roman remains in London, and in many cases when Roman remains are found they are either damaged or hidden or moved.

The temple of Mithras famously discovered in Walbrook Street in the 1950s was moved for an office block to be built. Earlier redevelopments were often unsympathetic – but not always. In medieval London, money and time could be saved by incorporating Roman work into a new building – which explains why there are more sections of London's Roman wall that survive than one might imagine. The difficulty is that they often form part of basement walls and are not open to the public.

However, a remarkable and little-known Roman survivor – unique in London – is the mosaic floor of a Roman house, which was incorporated into the church of All Hallows by the-Tower. All Hallows is the oldest church in the City of London but, despite surviving the Great Fire, it was severely damaged by German bombers and only its tower and outer walls survived. Apart from the mosaic in the Undercroft, the church is also home to another fascinating survivor from the earliest church on the site – a splendid seventh-century arch that incorporates Roman tile work. The Roman pavement, comprising fine red tesserae that look almost as bright today as they must have looked when they were first laid, is largely undamaged.

CUTTING THE RIBBON

1133

The long tradition of opening new buildings, shows and events by cutting a ribbon has its origins in London's long-vanished Cloth Fair. Cloth Fair was a medieval fair, dating from the twelfth century, that took place each year for three days, starting at the end of St Bartholomew's Day (24 August).

The Fair was held on the Smoothfield (the name Smithfield is a corruption of the original) just outside the old city gates, and it was the place where merchants met to buy and sell cloth. The fair was always opened by the Lord Mayor of London, who ceremoniously cut a piece of cloth to indicate that trading had begun, and this is why, centuries after the fair came to an end, this tradition is still used.

The land around St Bartholomew's Church where Cloth Fair was held was owned by the family of Lord Rich. Rich has gone down in history as the man who perjured himself to ensure that Thomas More was executed for refusing to acknowledge that Henry VIII was head of the Church in England. The houses in the little lane that is now known as Cloth Fair included, until 1917, several houses that dated from Lord Rich's time, but alas they were swept away at the end of the First World War. Two heavily restored seventeenth-century houses remain. Interestingly, one or two drapers and cloth merchants remained here until the beginning of the twentieth century.

MEDIEVAL CONDUIT

1240s

Medieval London drew its water from the Thames, but as the river became dirtier people began to complain that their ale (beer was a later invention relying on imported German hops) began to taste unpleasant, so a decision was made to bring water to the city via conduits (underground channels) that tapped into streams and underground springs on the northern hills of Hampstead and Highgate.

Lamb's Conduit Street in Holborn recalls a water supply repaired in 1564 by Sir William Lamb. The Holborn conduit supplied water from a dam created in the upper reaches of the old Fleet River. You can still see what's left of the old Lamb's Conduit Head – the remnants were incorporated into the wall of a 1950s building at the corner of Long Yard and Lamb's Conduit Street.

An even more ancient conduit was the Great Conduit that ran from Tyburn – modern Marble Arch – through wooden pipes all the way to the City. The route it took was across fields to Charing Cross then along the Strand and Fleet Street and thence to the City. The Great Conduit was built in the 1240s and the miles of conduit meant the water eventually reached a small stone building where citizens would take their buckets to fill. Nothing of the Great Conduit remains (it ceased to be used after the Great Fire of 1666) although occasionally, when work is being carried out along its old route, stretches of wooden pipe are discovered.

If you want to see the best-preserved conduit head in London, however, you'll need to go to Myddelton Passage in Islington. Here you will find the fourteenth-century Chimney or Devil's Conduit, which stood in Queen Square, Bloomsbury, until about 1912. The origins of its name are mysterious, but a remarkable photograph taken in 1912 shows the water still streaming along a channel down a stone slope inside the conduit and heading towards the City, which it had supplied for more than 600 years.

Unfortunately, this fascinating piece of history fell victim to the developers and it was destroyed, but at least the building that had allowed access to the stream at this point was preserved. It was taken to Islington in 1927 and rebuilt, and today it can be seen behind an office building. It is made of Portland stone and has a flat roof and upper and lower chambers. The stone construction – rather than cheaper timber or brick – shows how important piped water was to the City more than five centuries ago. The Chimney Conduit is said to have been an extension of the even more ancient White Conduit, which once brought water to Greyfriars monastery, later Christ's Hospital on Newgate Street.

COAL CELLAR CRYPT

1253

A vast amount of London's history remains hidden beneath later buildings. The city is so multi-layered that in places you would need to dig down 6–10ft (1.8–3m) to reach the level on which the Romans lived.

This is especially true within the City of London, which has been inhabited for so much longer than outlying regions, such as the Strand to the west and, east of the city, the hamlets beyond the Tower of London. But Fleet Street runs a close second in this respect. Just outside the western gate of the City along the river there were several large convents and priories. The name of Blackfriars Bridge, which crosses the River Thames at the point roughly where the old River Fleet would have run into it, harks back to the foundation of the black friars, or Black Freres, Dominican friars who established their priory here in 1276. A little further to the west, along Fleet Street, the Whitefriars (who wore white habits) established their Carmelite priory in 1253.

Until the end of the nineteenth century it was assumed that, following the destruction of both the Blackfriars and Whitefriars priories in 1540 as part of Henry VIII's Dissolution of the Monasteries, nothing of them remained. Then, during building work in the 1980s, a remarkable discovery was made. Beneath later buildings in what is now Magpie Alley, workmen discovered the almost perfectly preserved Whitefriars crypt.

Though preserved, the crypt was moved several feet from its original site and an office block was built on top. But if you go down the steps at the end of Magpie Alley you can see the crypt, which is now contained in a glass box.

CARMEN APPROVAL

1277

Many of London's old city livery companies are still well known, despite the fact that most now have little connection with the trade they once governed. The Goldsmiths' Company, the Mercers' Company and the Fishmongers', among others, all run charitable foundations, but they no longer regulate fishing or jewellery-making. One livery company, however, which is among the most ancient, does at least still carry out an annual rite that has been part of London life since the thirteenth century.

The fellowship of Carmen – or carriers – began in 1277 and their aim was to regulate the trade of keeping the streets of London clean as well as carrying goods. By the early sixteenth century they were known as the Fraternity of St Katharine the Virgin and Martyr of Carters. They set up locations where carts could be hired – called carrooms – and of course they regulated prices and conditions of hire. All licensed vehicles were to be marked appropriately and by the mid-nineteenth century there were more than 600 licensed carts in London and around 90 carrooms.

The arrival of the motor car and the lorry heralded the end of the old company of Carmen and by the 1960s hardly any carts remained in London. The few remaining carrooms were demolished – with one exception. It is at this carroom – a new place for it is chosen every year – that the Fraternity still marks a few carts each year. The event is usually held in the summer and dozens of horse-drawn carts and buses, as well as motor lorries, are brought together and branded – marked on a wooden plate using a hot iron – by the keeper of the Guildhall, before everyone retires for a celebratory lunch. The ceremony, though it no longer has any practical purpose, is a reminder that carrying goods has always, one way and another, been vital to the prosperity of London.

SARACEN'S HEADS

c.1300

A curious tale surrounds the popularity of pubs in London (and elsewhere) with the name 'Saracen's Head'. This ancient name dates back to the thirteenth and fourteenth centuries when soldiers returning from failed crusades found themselves without employment and in many cases set up as innkeepers. Among these veterans there was a feeling that their defeats were somehow rather ignominious, so to make it less embarrassing, those who set up pubs and inns made sure that the Saracen's Head part of the painting on their signs was huge and monstrous.

The idea was that such great and terrifying creatures were so awesome that no ordinary mortal ever had a hope of defeating them. The returning soldiers had effectively set up a series of advertisements explaining their defeat as something that was no discredit to them in the slightest!

THE BONE COLLECTION

1320

When the Victorian buildings that comprise Spitalfields Market, just east of the City, were being redeveloped in the 1990s, there was a real danger that the whole area would be obliterated and turned into yet more dull, monotonous (but probably iconic) office blocks. A compromise of sorts was reached between the developers and those interested in preserving as much as possible of London's historic fabric. As a result, the Victorian market buildings remain, together with a mix of new buildings.

During work on Bishop's Square, a remarkable and bizarre discovery was made. Beneath what had once been the graveyard of the long-demolished monastic foundation of St Mary Spital, from which the market gets its name, a remarkably well-preserved charnel house dating from around 1320 was discovered. A charnel house is rather like a crypt, but used to hold the bones of the dead. The charnel house or ossuary at Spitalfields appears to have been built 30 or 40 years after the foundation of the priory itself; it was the crypt of the chapel of St Mary Magdalene and St Edmund the Bishop, part of the priory foundation.

When rediscovered in 1999, the charnel house still contained countless bones. Rather than allowing the developers to destroy it or arrange to have it moved elsewhere, the decision was taken to incorporate the charnel house into the new office building, and it can now be viewed by appointment via a special basement.

As work went ahead to preserve the charnel house, thousands of other burials were discovered in what had been the surrounding graveyard and later the gardens of the Georgian terraced houses. It was traditional in graveyards to bury the dead and then gradually move across the graveyard filling the space. When the space had been filled, the gravediggers would return to the oldest side of the graveyard, remove the old graves and store the bones in a charnel house. It was regarded as a way to reuse the space while treating the remains with respect.

St Mary Spital was one of London's largest priories. When built it would have been on the edge of the City, with fields and scattered farms away to the east. When the priory was closed by Henry VIII in 1539, the crypt and chapel were not destroyed but adapted for use as a house. The last buildings were demolished at the beginning of the eighteenth century and new houses rose above it. A century later, no one recalled what lay beneath the gardens of those houses, but now this part of London's history has been revealed and preserved for posterity.

CROSS-DRESSING KING

1327

No one knows for sure, but Edward II is thought to have been homosexual. And it was his close, almost obsessive friendship with the nobleman Piers Gaveston that led to his abdication and, later, death.

Edward was so besotted with Gaveston that he promoted him above all the most powerful barons in the land, and it was a slight they would never forgive or forget. Edward was born in 1284, and reigned from 1307 until 1327.

One very curious fact is that if Edward's elder brother had lived, England would have had a King Alphonso (as Edward's brother was called) instead. Edward's biggest problem was that he put friendships with young men above affairs of state. His passion for Piers Gaveston, and later for the Despenser family, led eventually to war with Roger Mortimer, one of the most powerful figures in fourteenth-century England.

Among the extraordinary stories that circulated about Edward, both during his lifetime and afterwards, was that when he was alone he liked to dress in his wife's clothes. An ambassador in London saw him dressed in this way and merely commented that the king enjoyed a 'jest that would confuse any courtier in Europe'.

Such eccentric behaviour would not have led to serious problems on its own – effective and decisive monarchs were pretty much allowed to do as they pleased – but when

Edward alienated many of his nobles by confiscating their land and then lost the support of his wife, his authority was seriously damaged.

His queen, Isabella, left him in 1325 and returned to France. By 1326, she had almost certainly become involved in a relationship with the exiled Mortimer, and with him she returned from France in September 1326 at the head of an army, having decided to depose Edward and place her son (also called Edward; the name Alphonso had clearly been something of an anomaly) on the throne. The King's nobles quickly turned against him and he fled to Wales where he was captured. He was imprisoned in Berkeley Castle and quietly murdered in 1327, although there are suggestions that he managed to escape.

NAME OF THE ROSE

1381

Many ancient London ceremonies may seem rather pointless today, but the English have a great love of tradition – indeed, the stranger it is, the more they seem to enjoy it!

One of the most delightful ceremonies that still takes place in the city is known as the Knollys Rose Ceremony. The story behind the ceremony begins as long ago as 1381 with Sir Robert Knollys (c.1320–1407), a resident of Seething Lane near the Tower of London, friend of the king and powerful figure generally in city politics. Like all knights in medieval England, Sir Robert was a military man who could be called upon at any time to fight for his king. This duly happened and Sir Robert was called away to the wars with John of Gaunt. Military wives were used to being left for long periods at this time, which was just as well as Sir Robert was away for more than two years.

During that time, cloistered at home and no doubt rather bored, Lady Knollys found herself irritated by large amounts of chaff (corn husks) blown to her house from a threshing yard nearby. In fact she became so annoyed that she decided to do something about it. She offered a large sum to buy the threshing yard and, having secured it, immediately gave orders to her servants that it should be turned into a garden. But there was a problem. Lady Knollys' house was separated from the garden by Seething Lane itself, and at that time the lane was filled with mud, horse manure and probably the odd dead dog and cat. Without consulting anyone, Lady Knollys employed a carpenter to build a bridge over Seething Lane so that she could reach her new garden without getting her feet muddy or having to weave her way through the hoi polloi. The bridge over the lane antagonised the neighbours, who saw its construction as an act of arrogance on Lady Knollys' part, since she had not enquired before building if any of her neighbours might object.

Eventually the local authorities were drawn into the row and they felt that the Knollys should be reprimanded – but how was this to be done? Sir Robert was a powerful figure and the city officials could not risk upsetting him over the matter of the bridge, especially as he was away on the king's wars when it was built. They came up with a cunning solution: Lady Knollys was fined a single rose every year in perpetuity. The rose had to come from the Seething Lane garden and be presented to the Lord Mayor.

It was a delicate diplomatic fine that appeased the neighbours and charmed rather than upset the Knollys. The bridge of course is long gone, but the right to build it in theory remains so long as the rent continues to be paid – and it has been paid every year since the fourteenth century. The single rose is cut from the Seething Lane garden, placed on a cushion from All Hallows by the Tower church and carried in state to the Mansion House where it is presented to the Lord Mayor. It is known as a quit rent – a sort of land tax.

THE VANISHED INN

1390

Barnard's Inn, which was founded in 1252 as a school for law students, once took up a large area of land between Fetter Lane and Holborn. A seventeenth-century timber-framed and jettied façade looked out over Fetter Lane for centuries, but bombs and redevelopment destroyed these once magnificent buildings long ago, and it would be easy to assume that nothing of Barnard's Inn survives.

In fact, through a narrow alleyway off Holborn, almost completely surrounded by ugly modern buildings, yet largely intact, stands the late fourteenth-century hall of this ancient Inn of Court. Astonishingly, much of its original fabric survives, including the magnificent crown post and collar purling roof structure and sixteenth-century linenfold panelling. The elaborate timber structure that supports the roof was typical of many late medieval London houses, but this is the only remaining example in London. Even more extraordinary is the fact that the chalk-and-tile wall at the southern end of the building is almost certainly Roman work. Barnard's Inn as a lawyers' inn is long gone, but their building has provided a home for Gresham College since 1991 and is now used for meetings and dinners. Gresham College is itself a remarkable survivor, having organised free lectures and talks in London for more than four centuries.

GRASSHOPPER RESCUE

1565

Visitors to London are often baffled by a large golden grasshopper that sits on top of what used to be the City's most important commercial building – the Royal Exchange. The present mid-Victorian building was altered in 2001 but enough of the original fabric survives to make the building well worth a visit.

But what of the grasshopper? Well, the Royal Exchange was founded by financier Sir Thomas Gresham in 1565. Gresham was a brilliant banker who wanted somewhere in London for merchants to meet to buy and exchange goods and services. For more than a century after it was built, the Royal Exchange specifically excluded stockbrokers on the grounds that they were loud, uncouth and untrustworthy, which is a curious reflection on how little has changed since those days.

The first notable member of the Gresham family entered history in the 1200s. He was Sir Roger Gresham and the story goes that he was abandoned as a baby in a field in Norfolk and would have died but for the fact that the noise of a cricket singing attracted the attention of a passer-by, who came into the field and found him. The golden grasshopper commemorates that family legend and it also appears as part of the crest of Gresham College in Norfolk, which was founded in 1555 by another Gresham – Sir John.

The school was set up using funds and income from property stolen by Henry VIII from the Augustinian Priory at nearby Beeston Regis. The story of the boy saved by the noisy grasshopper is a rather nice one, but it is more likely that the grasshopper connection is rather more prosaic. The grasshopper is almost certainly just a visual pun on the Middle English word for grass – 'gres' (as in Gresham).

GARDEN OF EARTHLY DELIGHTS

c.1600

Buckingham Palace is one of the most famous buildings in the world and its history is well known. Less well known, however, is its garden, which extends to 42 acres (17 hectares) – the biggest in London – and has a remarkable wealth of wildlife, including an extraordinary number of moth species.

Pride of place among the trees and plants is an ancient mulberry tree planted, it is said, during the reign of James VI of Scotland and I of England (1566–1625), which serves as a reminder of one of the oddest periods in English history.

When silk first reached England from China it was considered to be such a wonderful material that plans were quickly hatched to find the secret to how it was made. Eventually it was discovered that the material came from the silkworm, although when this was first explained many scientists were outraged that anyone could be fooled by such an unlikely explanation. Eventually, however, the silkworm was confirmed as the source of the thread and entrepreneurs began to hope it might be possible to produce the wonderful new material in England. Travellers were quizzed about silk making on the other side of the world and the basic facts of the business were pieced together. Key to any hope of breeding and keeping silkworms was finding out what they ate, and when it was realised that mulberry trees were vital, a programme of frenzied planting began.

But, in their ignorance, those early plantsmen failed to realise that silkworms need white mulberry trees, not black mulberries. So almost all the mulberry trees planted in England in the early seventeenth century, including the one in the garden of Buckingham Palace, were the wrong type for silkworms, but they did produce the most wonderful fruit. The other strange thing about Buckingham Palace is that the River Tyburn flows right underneath it!

KATHERINE'S PILLAR
1628

It is often assumed that London was never a beautiful city like Florence or Rome. Somehow commercial success has fooled people into believing that one of the world's great capital cities was always a place of purely functional architecture – with a few notable exceptions, such as St Paul's Cathedral. This, of course, is entirely wrong and both the City of London and the area outside the ancient jurisdiction of the square mile were once very beautiful indeed in architectural terms.

  Anyone who has seen Crosby Hall, the stone mansion moved in the 1920s from the City to Chelsea, will realise that the City of London was once a wonderful combination of elaborate, timber-framed houses and highly decorated stone mansions. Many vanished in the Great Fire of London in 1666, it is true, but much survived only to succumb to the Victorian obsession with so-called 'improvement' where streets were widened and whole districts razed. The idea of preserving beautiful early buildings was simply unheard of. German bombers also destroyed a great deal that had survived, but perhaps the worst damage of all was inflicted by architects and planners during the 1960s and 1970s; indeed far more early buildings were lost during this period than in the whole of the Second World War. Most of the city's churches we see today, though described as being designed by Wren or Hawksmoor, are not really authentic at all –

they were rebuilt after suffering bomb damage of various degrees of severity. In many instances the whole church apart from the external walls had to be recreated. But one church survived the Great Fire, the war, the developers and the 1960s – St Katherine Cree in Creechurch Lane near Houndsditch.

Completed in 1628 (apart from the tower, which dates from more than a century earlier), the church was built on the site of the Augustinian Priory of Holy Trinity, Aldgate. St Katherine Cree was built to minister to the parishioners of Aldgate after the destruction of the priory following the Dissolution of the Monasteries that took place between 1536 and 1541. There is some evidence to suggest that the present church was built in the old priory burial ground and may even have been used as a mortuary while the priory still existed. The church we see today – it takes its curious name, 'Cree', from a corruption of the words 'Christ's Church' – is remarkable not just for its survival against all the odds, but also for the fact that it reveals, perhaps better than any other building, how London was built one layer upon another. Inside the main door to the church and a little to the right, visitors will see the top – the capital – of a pillar. Below the capital there is only around 2ft (0.6m) of the pillar itself. Why is this? The answer is that as the floor of the church has been built up bit by bit over the centuries, the pillar has become submerged and now only this top section remains visible. It is a remarkable example of how quickly layer succeeds layer in an ancient city. Another oddity can be seen on the wall in the lane outside: an eighteenth-century sundial (it may actually be rather earlier) now tells the time only for a short period each day. When it was first put here, the sun shone on it for long enough for passers-by to check the time, but as the lane has narrowed over the centuries and higher buildings have been erected, the sundial has become obsolete.

BEATING THE RIVER

c.1650

All Hallows by the Tower is London's oldest church, although much that we see today represents post-war reconstruction. The church, which was probably founded in the seventh century, is also the starting place for one of the city's most unusual ceremonies, known as 'beating the bounds'.

English villages across the country still beat the bounds each spring, and wherever you go, from Lincolnshire to Cornwall, from Herefordshire to Kent, you will find parishes that still take part in this ancient custom. Its purpose is to reassert and confirm all the land that falls within a particular parish. This was far more important in the past than it is now because maps were rudimentary and often inaccurate. Also, on the basis that good fences make good neighbours, it was always a good idea to remind people every year exactly who owned what and where.

Beating the bounds at All Hallows may well date back to the time when this was still a rural area. Generally speaking, beating the bounds ceremonies usually took place on Rogation days (days of prayer and fasting) but at All Hallows the ceremony takes place on Ascension Day. Masters of various livery companies take part as well as the clergy, and at various points around the parish the ground is beaten with canes.

It is said that until the mid-seventeenth century beating the parish's southern boundary included rowing to the middle of the river (the parish's southern boundary) and beating the river with canes.

A similar ceremony used to be carried out by officials from the Fishmongers' Company, one of the 12 Great Livery Companies of the City of London, and one of the oldest City Guilds. In medieval times they ritually beat the waters of the Thames to remind the fish that they were essential to life in London. The practice ended as London's river became so polluted that all fishing ceased and the fishmongers had to get their catch from further downstream and out to sea.

HERB STREWER

c.1660

Until the end of the nineteenth century, London and its inhabitants stank. Visitors were shocked at the state of the streets, the smell of the drains and cesspits and the rank odours that rose from over-filled parish churchyards, where the dead were often left just inches under the soil.

Monarchs were to some extent protected from the worst street smells, and since they could afford unlimited amounts of perfume they were at least able to disguise their own lack of hygiene. (Baths were considered eccentric and even dangerous until the end of the eighteenth century.)

Pomanders of various sorts were carried by the rich when they travelled in litters or carriages through the streets of London. Often these would be oranges spiked with nutmeg and were wafted under the nose. As part of the general attempt to protect themselves from noxious odours, the royal family, at some time in the sixteenth or seventeenth centuries, decided to create the post of 'Herb Strewer'.

The first herb strewer for whom there is any record was Bridget Rumney, who, as her title suggests, strewed herbs for more than a decade in the royal apartments for Charles II, for the princely sum of £12 per year plus 2 yards (1.8m) of scarlet cloth.

When George III was crowned in 1760, Mary Dowle was there to throw scented herbs in front of the royal entourage, and the tradition was still going strong in 1820 when George

IV was crowned. The title seems to have become hereditary by this time, so it may be that Mary Dowle died childless, as the next herb strewer on record is one Anne Fellowes.

Anne was appointed by George IV just before his coronation. Rather than being lowly servants, holders of the title had now become rather grand friends of the monarch, but the title as a practical job seems to have died with George IV, since no coronation since his has included the services of a herb strewer. However, the Fellowes family are certain that the title remains with them, and it is given to the eldest daughter in each generation.

PEPYS'S WALKWAY

1662

St Olave Hart Street is one of only a few medieval churches that still exist in the City. It is also the City's smallest church. Unfortunately, like so many London churches, its interior was largely destroyed by a German firebomb. However, the church still retains much that is of interest, including a memorial on the wall that marks the position of a door, specially built by the great seventeenth-century diarist Samuel Pepys, who worshipped here with his wife Elisabeth.

Both Pepys and his wife are also buried in the churchyard. By his own admission Pepys slept through many services, but he liked to attend church to ogle any young women who happened to be there. In fact, one young woman disliked the attention so much that she stuck a pin in him!

Pepys worked at the Navy Board nearby and he hated to get wet, so he had a covered walkway, staircase and door built so he could get from his desk to his pew in one of the St Olave's galleries (long gone) without having to go outside and risk the weather.

Another curious tale from St Olave's (the church is named after a Norwegian saint) concerns William Penn, the father of the founder of Pennsylvania. Penn spotted that St Olave's was in danger of being burned during the Great Fire of 1666, so he roused dozens of men from the naval dockyards nearby and they pulled down the houses surrounding the church, an act which saved it from destruction.

IT'S THE PITS

1665

If the stories are to be believed there is hardly an acre of London that was not once a plague pit filled with the skeletons of those who died of a disease that, according to some estimates, killed one-third of the population of Europe.

The Cumberland Hotel at Marble Arch is a good example, and though this was probably not a plague pit, thousands of skeletons were discovered when the foundations of the hotel were being dug at the beginning of the twentieth century. It is likely these bodies were some of the tens of thousands hanged over the centuries at nearby Tyburn. But one massive and genuine plague pit certainly does exist in Aldgate, and it gave the planners and engineers involved in building the underground railway a few headaches (but thankfully that was the least of their afflictions).

Aldgate (which actually means 'old gate') was at one time the main eastern entry and exit into the old City of London. It would have made sense, therefore, to take plague victims just outside the city walls and bury them there. Taking them any further would have been difficult because at the height of the plague the population of London was so devastated that hardly a soul could be found to move the dead anywhere.

So perhaps the discovery of thousands of bodies under what was planned to be Aldgate Station on the District Line should have come as no surprise. There were far too many to be removed and given proper burials elsewhere and planners in the late nineteenth and early twentieth century had no intention of letting a few bodies get in the way of progress, so the station was simply built in the middle of the plague pit. To this day, if you were to dig through the tunnel walls into the surrounding earth, you would soon come across the remains of London's plague victims.

BEST OF BROMLEY

1666

For centuries in England there was a tradition that wealthy men and women left much of their money to found groups of houses for the poor. Many of these houses still exist in many parts of the country – beautiful examples can be found at Abingdon in Oxfordshire and at Harefield in Middlesex, on the edge of what is now Greater London. A beautiful group of almshouses also survives in Acton on Churchfield Road.

These early nineteenth-century cottages were funded by a member of the Goldsmith's Company and though much altered (and no longer used for the purpose for which they were built) they are a reminder that London was once rich in such developments.

The oldest group of such houses in the whole country, still used for their original purpose, is in fact hidden away in the London suburb of Bromley. Bromley College was founded in 1666 by the Bishop of Rochester, John Warner, for the express purpose of providing accommodation for 'twentie poore widowes of orthodox and loyal clergy'. To this day the college still houses the widows of clergymen using its charitable foundation.

KING'S EGG

1670

The monarch and his or her family has always existed, in part at least, so that the general populace had something to look up to, with the royal family traditionally represented as a moral exemplar for ordinary mortals.

But this perception has often been an ambiguous one as, until relatively recently, almost every head of state has been, from a moral point of view, a pretty poor role model. Monarchs did their best to circumvent the problem by being as discreet as possible about their mistresses and their affairs, thereby giving the general public the impression that royalty lived by the highest standards.

Edward VII is a case in point – he happily slept with his friends' wives and at any one time he had four or five mistresses on the go. Charles II was even more profligate – he had so many mistresses he named streets after them to keep them happy and made their children (his illegitimate offspring) dukes, earls and lords. Visitors to St James's will discover that at least one street still bears the name of one of Charles II's favourite mistresses. This is Cleveland Row, a narrow street of eighteenth-century houses named after Barbara Palmer, Countess of Castlemaine, later Duchess of Cleveland, during the latter part of the seventeenth century.

WHAT'S IN A NAME?

1672

One of London's most ancient thoroughfares, the Strand – meaning a stretch of land by the water – was once the site of numerous mansions and palaces. It was just half a mile (0.8km) or so from the entrance to the City of London at Ludgate, but far enough away to allow the aristocracy to enjoy the fresh air and open space – and there was less risk of contracting the plague here on its periodic arrivals to the dense and crowded city.

One aristocrat who owned land along the Strand was George Villiers, 2nd Duke of Buckingham (1628–87). Villiers was part of the 'Merry Gang', which included the most notorious rake of the Restoration era, John Wilmot, 2nd Earl of Rochester.

Villiers was an amusing man but constantly fighting and womanising, to the extent that on several occasions he was imprisoned in the Tower of London. Each time he was released because Charles II enjoyed his company and had spent some of his time in exile in the company of Villiers.

When Villiers needed money – which, with his gambling and womanising, he frequently did – he sold his possessions. Eventually, in 1672, he sold his house and land along the Strand. York House, a grand residence overlooking the Thames just to the east of where Charing Cross Station now stands, had been owned by the Villiers family for generations.

Villiers sold up but could not bear the idea that his name would be forgotten in the area, so the builder who planned to demolish York House and lay out a new grid of streets was told that one condition of the sale was that every part of the duke's name had to be incorporated into the new street names.

This is the reason that today you will find a street running down the side of Charing Cross Station called Villiers Street. Nearby you will also find George Street, Buckingham Street and Duke Street. Villiers also had to have a little fun and when he saw that the word 'of' (remember, his full title was 'George Villiers, Duke of Buckingham') had not been included in the street names, he insisted that the deal was off unless there was a road or street called 'Of'. A compromise was reached and a narrow alley off Villiers Street became and remained until recently 'Of Alley'. It was renamed York Place in the twentieth century, but after a huge campaign of protest the sign carrying the new name also included the line 'Formerly Of Alley'.

PRIVATE STEPS

1675

If anyone has given the British legal system a bad name – and heaven knows there are many candidates – it is the famous Judge Jeffreys (1645–89). The son of an aristocratic Welsh landowner, Jeffreys studied at Cambridge and then entered Inner Temple, one of London's ancient Inns of Court, where he trained as a lawyer. He became a High Court Judge and it was not long before he gained notoriety for his utter ruthlessness. Even during his lifetime there was disquiet among the legal profession about his methods, but he usually did the king's bidding and was therefore quickly promoted and eventually raised to the peerage.

It was said that there was only one person in the kingdom of whom Jeffreys was afraid – and that was his wife. They were popularly known as 'St George and his dragon'. In 1685, after the Monmouth Rebellion (an attempt to overthrow the Catholic James II), Jeffreys presided over the Bloody Assizes, when hundreds of those who were associated with Monmouth were executed, often on flimsy evidence.

Widely hated, Jeffreys was much loved by the king despite the fact that Jeffreys himself hated Catholics. James even allowed Jeffreys to build a set of steps from his house into the then private grounds of St James's Park. Until the 1920s the steps still stood halfway along Storey's Gate, close to Parliament Square, and until they were demolished it was tradition to spit on them as you passed!

RULE-BREAKING SCHOOL

1679

Visitors to Westminster Abbey often forget that the large area around the abbey that is cunningly hidden by a high, ancient wall is actually a school. But this is no ordinary school. Westminster School (officially The Royal College of St Peter in Westminster) has educated at least seven prime ministers, as well as poets John Dryden and Ben Jonson, author A.A. Milne, architect Sir Christopher Wren and philosopher Jeremy Bentham. What makes the school so odd, however, is that, in addition to exclusively educating the very wealthy, the school has a dark, murderous past.

In 1679, a group of boys from the school killed a bailiff, but such was the elite nature of the school that its headmaster managed to get the boys off scot-free by paying a fine – the cost of which was then passed on to all the boys' parents. Ben Jonson also murdered a man but escaped hanging by pleading in Latin – an ancient rule that allowed murderers who could read to escape the noose. They were instead branded with a hot iron on the thumb, which is what happened to Jonson.

The school has its own private square and the students are housed in some of central London's most beautiful and ancient buildings – none of which can be visited by the general public. Perhaps most interesting of all is the eighteenth-century mansion hidden inside the school walls. Other ancient buildings here include a fourteenth-century college hall, an eighteenth-century college dormitory and early seventeenth-century Ashburnham House.

The school also includes England's oldest continually cultivated garden, its own rifle range and the use of Westminster Abbey as the school chapel. The happy tradition of criminality continued into the twenty-first century when, in 2005, the school was found guilty of the serious offence of running an illegal cartel with other expensive schools to keep its fees as high as possible.

One of the school's maddest customs is known as Greaze. Each year on Shrove Tuesday, a large pancake reinforced with horsehair (the Greaze) is thrown over an elevated bar, at which point the schoolboys fight for it for exactly one minute. The boy who tears off the biggest piece is traditionally given a golden sovereign (which he immediately gives back).

BOY ON A BASKET

c.1685

In Panyer Alley, near St Paul's Underground Station, is one of London's most delightful and overlooked monuments. Known as the Panyer Boy, this wall-mounted carving has been in the area since the 1680s and, wonderful though its survival is, due to continual redevelopment he has been moved up and down the same street at least four times.

The Panyer Boy is currently sited on a wall close to the steps into St Paul's Underground Station. The boy in the carving appears to be sitting on what looks like a bread basket (or 'pannier'), but the stone is now so eroded that it is difficult to be sure; it could even be a bale of wool or straw. At one stage the carving was locally known as 'pick my toe', because if you look at it from the right angle it looks as if the boy has simply sat down on the nearest comfortable object and started picking at one of his toes. The inscription beneath the boy tells us nothing about what he is doing. It reads:

When ye have sought the City round
Yet this is still the highest ground.

The wording is somewhat baffling because this street is definitely not the highest point in the City of London, and we can be pretty sure that there is a link between the sculpture and Panyer Alley because, so far as we know, the carving has always been somewhere in the alley. We also know that bread was sold here in medieval times; there was also a bread market in nearby St Martin's Le Grand.

However, the area has been rebuilt so many times that the ground has sunk and so has all the land round about. It could be that at the time the boy was made, this was the highest ground in the city or nearly so – certainly in the mid-nineteenth century, it was believed to be at least the second highest point after the standard on nearby Cornhill. After the Great Fire, when almost all the City was rebuilt in brick, Panyer Alley was a street of fine houses with shops underneath, and we know that the Panyer Boy was affixed to one of these houses. Later houses in the street, before the advent of office blocks, were demolished in the late nineteenth century, but when the new buildings went up the Panyer Boy was re-embedded in the new wall. The simplest explanation is probably that he is connected with the bread sellers formerly found here and perhaps also there is a connection with an old pub, The Panyer, that stood half-way along the alley. The part about the high ground, we can only guess at.

WOODEN SHOES CHURCH

1687

Very few London churches escaped the Blitz entirely unscathed. St Katherine Cree in Aldgate (see page 36) is one such example, but another, perhaps less well-known escapee is the curiously named St Margaret Pattens in Eastcheap.

There has been a church on this site since at least the eleventh century. The first was almost certainly a timber building and it was rebuilt in stone some time later, though the exact date is not recorded. That church fell into such a state of disrepair that it was demolished in the mid-sixteenth century, and its replacement was destroyed in the Great Fire. The church we see today, designed by Christopher Wren and built in 1687, is remarkable for a number of reasons, not least, of course, the sheer fact of its survival and escape from the Victorian modernisers.

But what about that peculiar name? St Margaret was and still is the guild church of the patten-makers. A patten is a type of overshoe that has no modern counterpart and disappeared so long ago that very few people know what it is. Pattens came in many shapes and styles, but were wooden shoes on short stilts. Usually they were slipped on over normal leather shoes, rather like a wooden sandal, but the wooden sole was supported by two 3in (7.6cm) wooden pillars. This meant that the wearer could walk London's filthy, muddy (and often dung-covered) streets while keeping his or her polished leather shoes clean. At St Margaret's, and elsewhere, pattens would have been taken off on Sunday mornings and left at the door.

A curious remnant of St Margaret's connection with the patten-makers can be seen in an old glass case beneath the church tower, where numerous examples of pattens dating back to the eighteenth century and earlier have been collected. The case also houses a number of odd-looking tools that were needed to carve wooden pattens – the whole structure was made from a single piece of wood to avoid the difficulty of firmly fixing the stilts to the wooden soles. An old sign inside the church still says, 'Will the Women remove their pattens before entering the Church'.

St Margaret's has several other wonderful and rare survivors. The eighteenth-century organ still has its eighteenth-century case (very rare in itself), and there are two canopied churchwardens' pews. These pews, with their high doors and covers, are unique, and remind us that in the past the inside of a church was used to make all sorts of social distinctions: the local aristocrats would often have their own pews where they would be shielded from having to view the great unwashed. But perhaps the strangest survivor inside St Margaret Pattens is the punishment box, a special pew where sinners were made to sit during services. This rare example even has a devil's head carved on it just to ram the message home!

The outside of the church is very odd too. It includes a 200ft (61m) spire but in a medieval design. No one knows why Wren chose this design, given that at the time the church was built, most things medieval were seen as crude and barbarous and architects slavishly followed the precepts of classical architecture. The gothic revival was still a century and more away, and yet in a rare eccentric moment Wren seems to have acknowledged that not all things gothic were necessarily bad. The spire is also unique as it is the only one of Wren's lead-covered timber spires to survive.

CHEPE HOUSES

c.1690

London's Cheapside was once one of Europe's most remarkable streets. A long row of fine houses that overlooked an ancient market (*chepe* was a Saxon word for a market) was destroyed first by the Great Fire of London in 1666, and in the twentieth century it was destroyed once again by German bombers and post-war developers. Today most of the street is hideous. But a curious tale links one of the few early buildings that remain in Cheapside and are built on a human scale.

In his *Survey of London* (1720), historian and biographer John Strype said that Cheapside was 'a very spacious street adorned with lofty buildings, well inhabited by goldsmiths, linen drapers, haberdashers and other great dealers'. At the corner of Wood Street there are three shops, just two storeys high, built by the parishioners of St Peter, West Cheap, in the late seventeenth century. No. 73 contains a staircase that formed part of the previous house on the site. Sir Christopher Wren is said to have built it for the Lord Mayor William Turner (1615–93).

The terms of the centuries-old lease on the buildings apparently forbids in perpetuity the building of anything higher than the existing buildings. For once the lawyers were on the side of protecting historic buildings – even they realised it would be very difficult to twist the terms of the lease to allow yet another monstrous carbuncle to be built on the site. An even more remarkable survivor is the enormous London plane tree that rises behind the little buildings. The tree marks the site of the old church of St Peter in Chepe, which was destroyed in the Great Fire. Modern, faceless office blocks loom over the part of the churchyard that remains and out of which the tree grows. This delightful corner has long intrigued artists. In the collection of poems that was to make William Wordsworth and his friend Samuel Taylor Coleridge famous – *Lyrical Ballads* of 1798 – there is a poem called 'The Reverie of Poor Susan'. Here the corner of Wood Street and Chepeside is recalled:

At the corner of Wood Street, when daylight appears
Hangs a Thrush that sings loud, it has sung for three
   years:
Poor Susan has passed by the spot, and has heard
In the silence of morning the song of the bird.

'Tis a note of enchantment; what ails her? She sees
A mountain ascending, a vision of trees;
Bright volumes of vapour through Lothbury glide
And a river flows on through the vale of Cheapside.

QUEEN MARY'S STEPS

1691

Westminster Hall, the Jewel Tower and the Banqueting House are well known to tourists and London residents alike. These are the last remnants of the vast old complex of buildings known as Whitehall Palace.

At its peak the buildings and courtyards of the old palace stretched from present-day Westminster Hall almost to Charing Cross, and halfway along what is now Whitehall was the Holbein Gate, a tall Tudor brick tower with a clock. The gatehouse tower that still stands at St James's Palace is very similar. A French visitor called Sorbière came to London in 1665 and noted that the Banqueting House, which still stands, was easily the greatest part of the old palace. The rest, he observed, was a hodgepodge of buildings from different periods and of different sizes which had been made contiguous by all sorts of haphazard means.

There were several courtyards and in these the public would gather to watch the king take his morning walk. Others were allowed to watch the king eat lunch. Indeed, the poor king was never allowed a moment's privacy – even when he went to the lavatory he was accompanied as, despite his many privileges, he was thought of as public property. The penalties for any attack on the sovereign were so severe – hanging, drawing and quartering, for example – that it was simply assumed the public would just gaze at the king in awe, and that no one would dream of attacking him – a very different situation from the one we know today where the royal family is kept as far away as possible from its subjects, and when they are allowed on walkabout security is tight.

Almost all the old palace burned down in 1698. As we have seen, the Jewel Tower and Banqueting House survived, but unbeknownst to most visitors to London, two other parts of the ancient palace still survive. The first is known as Queen Mary's Steps. The river wall of the Tudor part of Whitehall Palace was altered in 1691, when Christopher Wren built a terrace for Queen Mary, the wife of William of Orange, that overlooked the Thames. The terrace was a little less than 300ft (91.5m) long and projected around 70ft (21.3m) out into the river, which is difficult to imagine today because the river is around 300ft narrower than it once was because the embankment was built out in the late nineteenth century. At either end of Wren's terrace, beautifully curved steps led to the river so that William and Mary could walk down and step into the state barge. It was long thought that the steps had been destroyed along with the rest of the palace, but when a government office was being built at the site in the mid-twentieth century, the steps were uncovered and restored. Today the curved steps to the north can be seen together with a section of the terrace and the old river wall. Sadly, the steps at the southern end did not survive. Today you must view the site from the road as it is next to the main Ministry of Defence building, but the general layout and the sense that these are ancient stones are still clear.

The other fascinating part of the old palace that survives, but which is rarely seen, is Henry VIII's wine cellar. The cellar was built in 1536 to house the thousands of barrels of wine delivered from France each year for the use of the king and his court. Its beautiful vaulting surrounded by the damp of the ancient river deposits provided a cool destination for a commodity of enormous value at the time, but when the palace burned down and subsequent houses were built, and in their turn destroyed, the cellar was forgotten until, in 1949, when the new Ministry of Defence building was being built, it was rediscovered deep beneath the accumulated soil levels.

The cellar, which has much of the look of a medieval church crypt, is 70ft (21.3m) long and 30ft (9.1m) wide. It was intact when rediscovered and almost undamaged. Did the developers rejoice? Not a bit. They and the government cared little for the cellar and would have been unconcerned at its destruction but for the intervention of Queen Mary, the widow of George V, who asked that it be saved. Had it been anyone else it would have been likely that their request would have gone unheeded, but thanks to the royal plea the cellar was saved. But it was moved, not brick by brick, but wholesale. First an excavation was made all around it. The whole room was then encased in steel and concrete and lowered by 20ft (6.1m). It was also moved 10ft (3m) to the west of its original position. Only in Britain would the authorities make it almost impossible to see this wonderful historic relic – Ministry of Defence officials hold events in the cellar but, absurdly, no one else is allowed in!

HIDDEN MANSION

1693

As the City of London grew in wealth, it became increasingly commercial. As early as the Middle Ages, the wealthiest tried to escape its densely cluttered streets by building mansions along the Strand just outside the western gate – Ludgate. With the exception of the chapel of St John, nothing of these great mansions survives today, but the habit of moving westwards continued for centuries until, in the late seventeenth and early eighteenth century, London had reached Hyde Park in the west and north beyond what is now Oxford Street to Marylebone Road.

Oxford Street had formerly been the Tyburn Road, but the name was changed as it served as an unwelcome reminder that this was the route the condemned took to the Tyburn gallows where Marble Arch now stands. At first glance, it may appear that all the grand houses between Oxford Street and the Marylebone Road have long since vanished, but this is not the case. As the speculative builders moved in and the rich moved even further west and north, some of the great detached mansions were cunningly incorporated into new terraces for the middle classes. Nos. 100–103 Great Russell Street do not stand out from the houses either side, but this was once Thanet House, the home of Samuel Johnson's great friend, the eccentric Topham Beauclerk (1739–80).

Beauclerk is remembered today only for his friendship with the great author of the first truly comprehensive

English dictionary, but in his day he was a well-known wit and man about town – he was perhaps the only man Johnson would be afraid to take on in a contest. In Boswell's *Life of Dr Johnson*, Beauclerk is a central figure. Though querulous and eccentric, he shone in company in which he felt at ease, as we see in Boswell's famous book, and he loved jokes and play. On the downside, he is reputed almost never to have washed, but when he died Johnson said: 'This is a loss the whole nation cannot repair.' Johnson went on to say that 'No man was ever so free, when he was going to say a good thing, from a look that expressed that it was coming or when he had said it from a look that expressed that it had come.' Johnson concluded that Beauclerk's talents were 'those which he had felt himself most disposed to envy than those of any whom he had known'.

Like another great conversationalist – the twentieth century's Desmond MacCarthy – Beauclerk is now largely forgotten because his great talent lay in the spoken word, rather than writing; only in Boswell do we get a sense of how electrifying Beauclerk could be. Beauclerk lived at Thanet House in Great Russell Street for many years, but the house had actually existed a century before Beauclerk was born. It was remodelled in the eighteenth century but no doubt retained some deep structures from the earlier house. The list of aristocrats who once lived in this now-forgotten house is impressive: the house gets its name from the Earl of Thanet, who took a 62-year lease in 1693. Sir Thomas Coke, later Viscount Coke, lived here along with the Marquess of Tavistock, the Earl Bathurst and, intriguingly, Diana Spencer, an ancestor of the late Princess of Wales who was by contemporaneous accounts a talented painter. She eventually married Topham Beauclerk.

By the mid-nineteenth century, Thomas Cubitt, the great-great-grandfather of Camilla, Duchess of Cornwall, had been employed to remodel the front of the house again, but to this day it echoes its former incarnations.

Another grand house that once stood alone and splendidly isolated is Bourdon House in Davies Street just north of Mayfair. This five-bay, pedimented house faces south today into a garden bordered by Bourdon Street, but if you look carefully you will see that its design is distinct from the houses that now surround it. It may look like part of a group of houses, but it is actually a grand mansion preserved by the Dukes of Westminster who own all the land between here and Belgravia.

SCHOOL FOR SCANDAL

1700

Few private houses in London have such a rich and strange history as Walpole House in Chiswick. Built in the late seventeenth century, the house looks out across a narrow riverside street to the Thames. In its early days it was home to Barbara Villiers (1640–1709) for the last nine years of her life. She had been a great beauty of the time and was one of Charles II's favourite mistresses. After his death in 1685, a Puritan air settled over London and Villiers found herself banished from court. She was unhappy and decided to come to Chiswick, which was then a deeply unfashionable village, miles from London.

Soon after she took up residence, local residents regularly reported seeing her praying at an upstairs window by the light of the moon and, whatever the truth of the story, it is certain that in her final years she was a sad, embittered woman. She could never accept the loss of her beauty, nor her exile from court. She died at Walpole House and her misery was so great that it was said her ghost was regularly seen at the window; even into the twentieth century residents of the house occasionally reported hearing footsteps crossing empty rooms late at night. But Walpole House has other claims to fame.

Thomas Walpole, nephew of the Prime Minister Sir Robert, lived here from 1798–1803 and by the mid-nineteenth century it was a school for vagrant girls. The school became very well known – so much so that it was even visited by Queen Victoria. By the 1840s, Walpole House had changed hands again. It was now a boys' school, where the author William Makepeace Thackeray studied for a while, and it was this building that he immortalised (so it is claimed) as the dreadful Miss Pinkerton's Academy in his famous novel *Vanity Fair*.

WATERMAN'S REST

1700

London's Bankside retains a few glimpses of its ancient past. In Elizabethan times people crossed the river for pleasure, for Bankside and Southwark were famous for their brothels, or 'stews' as they were known. Respectable people lived north of the river and kept quiet about their regular visits to the stews over the water. The religious hypocrite who condemned the pleasures of the south bank while regularly enjoying the theatre, the cock pit and the brothels is a stock character in Elizabethan and Jacobean drama. Curiously, those of a pious disposition felt the theatre was even more pernicious than the brothel, which is why, in 1599, the King's Men – the company for whom Shakespeare wrote many of his plays – dismantled their theatre at Shoreditch on the edge of the city and, having carried it across London Bridge in a series of carts, rebuilt it close to where the modern Globe now stands.

The history of the Southwark stews and theatres is, of course, well known. Perhaps less well known is that much of the traffic that crossed the river was not carried by the bridge – London Bridge was then the only solid river crossing. Most people crossed by boat, and the watermen, one of London's most powerful guilds, manned the boats and did the rowing. Crossing London Bridge in a cart or carriage could take as long as an hour because it was so crammed with shops and houses that the traffic had to squeeze along a pathway just 6ft (1.8m) wide in places. It followed that those who wanted an evening of pleasure crossed by water. Only one physical relic of the watermen remains: an ancient stone seat now set into a modern building in Bear Gardens, close to the river. Legend has it that the seat is exactly where it would have been in the year 1700, when the watermen waiting to be asked to carry someone over the river would sit.

ON YOUR MARKS

1701

Bevis Marks Synagogue, close to that much-maligned London landmark, 30 St Mary Axe (also known as The Gherkin), is reasonably well known. It was completed in 1701 and has suffered only minor damage and alteration in the intervening years. Based on the great synagogue of Amsterdam, which was completed in the early 1670s, Bevis Marks is remarkable for being the only synagogue in Europe to have offered services continuously for more than 300 years.

Synagogues across Europe were frequently burned to the ground in regular uprisings against Jews, and even the great Amsterdam synagogue lost much of its interior after it was closed by the Nazis – the galleries were removed and used as firewood. But Bevis Marks soldiered on unscathed. Perhaps its most unusual feature is the massive ark in which the Torah scrolls are kept. Even on close inspection this looks like yellow marble, yet it is not – in fact, it is cunningly painted solid oak.

QUEEN ANNE'S ALCOVE

1705

At the Bayswater end of the Serpentine lake in Hyde Park is a curious shelter. Immensely tall and built of carefully cut stone, the shelter, which is open to the elements on one side, features fine oak panelling and a curved wooden seat. Many visitors sit here to enjoy the view across the ornamental ponds and fountains nearby but few realise that this unaltered and rather magnificent little building dates back to 1705.

At that time, it was situated a few hundred yards away, near Kensington Palace, but people felt that it attracted too many prostitutes and a plan was hatched to get rid of it. Outraged by this idea, a London builder called Mr Cowley, who loved the summerhouse, had it moved in 1867 to its present location. He paid for the move out of his own pocket and we should be grateful to him because without his action the summerhouse would almost certainly have been demolished.

The move took the structure away from the strait-laced royals in their grand palace and placed it on the edge of Hyde Park, well away from Kensington Palace. With its triangular pediment and twin alcoves (as well as Queen Anne's monogram), the summerhouse is rather grand, but what makes it even more remarkable is that it may well have been designed by the great Christopher Wren and is perhaps his least-known building.

INVISIBLE BARN

c.1710

The ancient gatehouse of St James's Palace still stares north up St James's Street, as it has done since Tudor times. Soon after the palace was first built, houses gradually sprang up along the road north towards what is now Piccadilly. Miraculously, one or two houses – including Lock & Co. Hatters – survive from the late seventeenth century.

Apart from two eighteenth-century gentlemen's clubs, the other buildings that line St James's date mostly from the end of the nineteenth century, their grand forms a reflection of what was seen as the power of a great empire, but take a left turn a short way up St James's Street into Blue Ball Yard and you will see a most remarkable survivor from the days when this area was home to the palace and its farms. The long, low building that fills two sides of the courtyard into which the alleyway opens looks remarkably like an old farm building from the early 18th century – and that is exactly what it is.

As the main St James's Street was redeveloped over the centuries, the farm to which this barn was once attached was forgotten, but it was certainly here in the seventeenth century when it was used to stable horses. It is an extraordinary piece of history.

COACHING INN

1720

When large areas of London began to be redeveloped in
the early twentieth century, and especially after the war, the
buildings that survived the wreckers tended to be pubs.

This is why you will often find a Victorian pub surviving
otherwise unscathed in a landscape of 1960s tower blocks.
Two of the most remarkable pub survivors actually take us
back beyond the Georgian era, to a time when the capital
relied heavily on post houses to keep the traffic moving on
the many turnpike roads that led out of the city.

The British term 'post office' comes from the inns that
were once dotted roughly a day's journey by horse apart
from one another on the main routes out of London. These
post houses were where a team of horses would be changed
– horses had to be changed regularly on a long journey if
the distance was to be covered in good time.

Against all the odds, a pub that was once part of this
network of post houses survives on the Bayswater Road in
west London. This looks much like any other road until you
look carefully. In fact, it is the old Tyburn Road, which ran
from the City via Holborn and Marble Arch (then Tyburn)
and on to the villages of Shepherd's Bush, Acton, Hanwell
and ultimately Oxford and beyond. The Swan pub at No. 66
is especially revealing of this area's history. Set back from
the road and overlooking Hyde Park, this coaching inn would
have been an early stop for the mail coaches from the city.

Eighteenth- and early nineteenth-century engravings show the pub looking remarkably as it does today, but isolated on what was once a road notorious for highwaymen. Hyde Park was then a dangerous place, where every tree might conceal a robber, so coaches would leave the Swan well armed, and those travelling on horseback would generally travel behind a carriage rather than risk the road alone.

The survival of The Swan, which was probably built in around 1720, is rather wonderful, but some of the tales told about it are entirely wrong. It is claimed that the condemned stopped here for a last drink on the way to the gallows at Tyburn, for example, but this is false. Condemned prisoners were brought to Tyburn from Newgate Prison and a journey from Newgate will reach Tyburn a good half-mile (0.8km) before it gets to The Swan. But stand outside the old pub and look up towards Marble Arch, and with open parkland on the right it is easier to imagine London's old coaching days here than anywhere else.

SICK IN PICTURES

1736–37

Most people have come across the work of William Hogarth (1697–1764), painter, satirist, social critic and cartoonist, but the great man's eccentricities are less well known.

His house at Chiswick escaped demolition and it is now bordered by the busy A4 that leads out of London towards Reading, but the interior and garden are much as Hogarth would have known. Especially eccentric is a wonderful device he created that allowed him to open his bedroom door to his servant without getting out of bed – it's a bell pull by the bedhead, attached to a pulley that runs across the ceiling and down to the bolt on the door. Hogarth's tomb also survives in the nearby churchyard, but sadly the church he knew was rebuilt (apart from the tower) in the 1800s.

He was such a popular artist that his pictures were widely engraved and disseminated via prints. He was a great patriot, and when he heard that an Italian artist had been asked to paint the walls of the staircase of the great hall at St Bartholomew's Hospital, he was so incensed he offered to do the work himself for nothing.

Understandably the authorities jumped at this opportunity to procure the work of the greatest artist of the day at no cost. Hogarth painted two main scenes – the Pool of Bethesda and the Good Samaritan. Most people think the pictures are murals and printed directly on to plaster but, in fact, they are painted on canvas and attached to the walls.

The Pool of Bethesda was painted in an artist's studio in St Martin's Lane near the present church of St Martin-in-the-Fields, but *The Good Samaritan* was painted from scaffolding specially erected for the artist in the hall itself. Both large-scale pictures were finished and in position by 1737, and are one of London's greatest artistic secrets.

The choice of *The Pool of Bethesda* comes from the Gospel of St John, which tells of a pool in Jerusalem known for its healing properties. The significance of *The Good Samaritan* painting needs no explanation, but what's curious about *The Pool of Bethesda* canvas is that many, if not most, of the models for the figures were patients at the hospital – one figure appears to have rickets, then a common complaint, another is blind, yet another arthritic, while another suffers from jaundice. It has even been suggested that one of the figures is suffering from a depressive disorder.

The paintings are still used as an educational tool as the symptoms of the various illnesses depicted are so accurate. Hogarth was very proud of these pictures and insisted on returning in the years after they were painted to personally clean them. He also insisted that they should never be varnished – his wishes were ignored and by the early twentieth century, when they were cleaned, they may have had as many as a dozen layers of varnish on them. Hogarth was born in St Bartholomew Lane, so he felt a special interest in this work, but nevertheless, he certainly spent a great deal of time and effort ensuring these are among his masterworks – despite not being paid a penny.

FOUNDLING'S ACORN

1739

Only the gatehouses survive of one of London's most remarkable eighteenth-century institutions – the Foundling Hospital, set up by philanthropist Thomas Coram (c.1668–1751) in 1739. Coram was horrified at the way children and babies were allowed to die in the streets of London. He spent nearly 20 years petitioning the government to do something about it, and at last a Royal Charter allowed the creation of the hospital, effectively the world's first orphanage, in open fields in Bloomsbury. Babies could be left anonymously in a specially designed alcove in one of the outer walls, and every child was taken in.

The Foundling Hospital survived on its Bloomsbury site, which is opposite Great Ormond Street Hospital, until the 1920s, when most of the buildings were demolished and the charity moved to Redhill in Surrey, where it continues to this day. You can still visit the Coram fields and see the gatehouses, and part of the outer wall and the grounds where the buildings once stood are now a children's play area.

The Coram Museum in Redhill includes a number of exhibits, including some of the pitiful items destitute mothers left with their babies when they were forced to abandon them. These items include a penny, a silver chain, and even – perhaps saddest of all – an acorn. Remarkably, the Foundling Hospital still has the records of more than 25,000 children who passed through its doors.

ART AND AFTERWARDS

1740

It is easy to forget that even great artists were once just ordinary mortals trying to make a living often in difficult conditions. The great J.M.W. Turner (1775–1851) rented a terraced house at 64 Harley Street, for example, and turned it into a shop to try to sell his paintings – the house, despite its associations, was demolished in the twentieth century.

More remarkable than Turner, however, is the story of the great Italian painter Giovanni Antonio Canal (1697–1768), better known as Canaletto. This name, Canaletto ('little canal'), was used to distinguish him from his father Bernardo Canal, who was also a painter.

Canaletto began his working life as a theatrical scene painter. He was also famous for using a camera obscura – a device that showed a reflection in a frame of the scene the artist wished to paint. This convinced Canaletto that distant figures were actually blurred and so he painted them as blobs. The effect was to create a new kind of shimmering realism.

What is not well known about Canaletto, however, is that he lived for some time in a small, rundown house in Soho, which still exists. Canaletto moved to London because his ability to earn a living depended on selling his paintings to the wealthy English who flocked to Venice as part of the Grand Tour undertaken by many aristocratic young men. When the War of the Austrian Succession began in 1740, fewer English visitors reached Venice and so Canaletto was in trouble. In an attempt to reach buyers on their home turf, therefore, he came to England, and here he lived at 41 Beak Street, Soho, where he met his clients and showed them his work. He stayed in England for around ten years, travelling continuously and painting the houses and castles of the rich, as well as scenes along the River Thames.

The biggest joke about Canaletto is that his style became so familiar and was copied to such a great extent by others that many critics have denounced genuine Canalettos as fakes painted by inferior artists.

SCANDAL AT THE
HORSE GUARDS
1750

If you stand on Horse Guards Parade, that magnificent square that leads to Whitehall on one side and St James's Park on the other, you instantly notice the white buildings straight ahead of you with their central archway (built by the great classical architect Inigo Jones) but look to the right and there is an equally distinguished-looking, white stone-fronted building with a prominent Venetian window. Now the London headquarters of the Scotland Office (staffed by civil servants responsible for Scottish affairs), this building was originally a private residence.

Built in the 1750s for Sir Matthew Fetherstonhaugh (pronounced 'Fanshaw'), the house was later occupied by Lord Montagu (at which time it became Montagu House); it was owned from 1788–92 by Prince Frederick, Duke of York, and from 1793–1830 by Lord Melbourne. It was at this point in the building's history that one of the great scandals of London life took place.

Lord Melbourne's son William had married Lady Caroline Lamb, who, on reading a new bestselling poem called 'Childe Harold's Pilgrimage' (by Lord Byron), declared that whatever the young poet looked like she simply had to meet him. And meet him she did. He almost certainly declared his love for her in this house in Whitehall, possibly in the famous rotunda – a large, ornate circular entrance hall unique in London and largely unaltered today. What Caroline didn't realise, however, was that Byron's protestations of love did not mean he would stay with her forever. Their passionate affair ended in a welter of recriminations and insults, which became far worse when Byron married Lady Caroline's cousin, Annabella Milbanke.

Caroline must have had an inkling that she tended to choose the wrong men as Byron was a notorious rake and her husband William seems to have been even worse. (Indeed, in a letter to her mother Caroline implied that he had unreasonable and unnatural sexual demands.) But Caroline and Byron's rows continued for years here in this house in Whitehall and elsewhere, reaching a pitch of intensity when she cut off all her pubic hair and sent it to him.

By 1830 the mad rants of Lady Caroline and her lover were long gone, and the house had been renamed Dover House after its last private owner, George James Welbore Agar-Ellis (Lord Dover). From 1830 until today Dover House has been the home of civil servants quietly devoted to Scottish affairs.

THEATRE GHOST

c.1750

Few London theatregoers realise that an evening in the theatre is often an evening among the dead. The Theatre Royal has a number of ghosts, but the strangest is 'The Man in Grey' who has been seen regularly for more than a century.

While most spirits and ghoulish apparitions tend to come out at night, the Man in Grey appears during daylight hours – more specifically, between 10a.m. and 6p.m. He haunts the oldest theatre in London while clothed in a long grey cloak and an old-fashioned, three-cornered hat of the type often worn by eighteenth-century gentlemen. On one occasion, more than 150 people in a matinée audience saw him simultaneously, although another hundred watching the same performance said they saw nothing at all. Some actors have said they've felt a pat on the back during a show, and Harry Secombe insisted he saw the ghost in his dressing room in the summer of 1960, when he was appearing in *The Four Musketeers*. Most importantly, this ghostly apparition always heralds a long and successful run, including *The King and I*, *Oklahoma*, *The Pirates of Penzance* and *Miss Saigon*.

The ghost may be linked to a gruesome discovery more than 150 years ago. In 1850, during rebuilding work at the theatre, the skeleton of a man with a dagger still embedded in his ribs was found in a previously unknown and long-bricked-up room. It is within feet of this site that the man most often makes his presence known, but nobody knows who he is.

GRAVE MATTERS
1751

In the eighteenth and earlier centuries London's graveyards were simply places where the dead were buried, but the Victorian love of the gothic and the macabre changed all that. Wreathed in dense fog and with increasingly elaborate tombs, London graveyards became the centre of a huge corpus of ghost stories.

In the mid-nineteenth century all the parish churchyards were closed in central London because they were full to bursting point, and frequent outbreaks of disease were attributed to the terrible state of these burial grounds. But one such area escaped the general closure, and the story surrounding its creation and continued existence is one of London's least-known tales.

The Moravian Burial Ground on the King's Road, Chelsea, was opened as long ago as 1751 on land provided free of charge by the leader of the Moravians in England, the splendidly named Count Nicholas Ludwig von Zinzendorf (1700–60). The Moravian Church was founded in Moravia, in what was then Bohemia in central Europe, in 1457. Its founder, Jan Hus, wanted the church to adopt more early Byzantine ideas, including married priests, no indulgences and a rejection of the idea of purgatory. The Moravians call themselves the Unity of the Brethren, but gained the name Moravians when they left Moravia for Saxony in the early eighteenth century to escape persecution. Eventually they established themselves in London, but they soon needed somewhere to bury their dead.

But how did their little graveyard in Chelsea escape the general prohibition of burials in London?

The explanation has to do with the Moravians' strange burial practices. Visitors to their burial ground will immediately notice that all the gravestones are the same size, and are all laid flat on the grass. The idea was to ensure that rich and poor, famous and obscure, were treated identically in death. But the habit that really let the Moravians off the legal hook was their practice of burying their dead very much deeper in the ground than the Anglican or Catholic Church.

For Catholics and Anglicans, a 6ft (1.8m) deep grave was quite enough and it was perfectly acceptable for further bodies to be piled on top of the first body once a few years had passed. The Moravians did not allow this system of multiple burials, and they also buried their dead at least twice as far down in the ground as any other Christian sect. Their graveyard was always a byword for cleanliness and hygiene and that is why it has remained open, in theory, to this day.

GARRICK UNDER THE ROAD

1756

Shakespeare's work was famously 'bowdlerised' or sanitised in the eighteenth century to try to make the gruesome endings more positive and his profanities less shocking. Thus *King Lear* was given a happy ending, with Cordelia surviving to live happily ever after.

The word *bowdlerise* comes from the writer Thomas Bowdler (1754–1825), who wanted to make Shakespeare more decorous so that it could be read aloud to a family without the risk of impropriety. But, despite this sense that Shakespeare was rude and vulgar, the Bard was particularly revered in the eighteenth century, and nowhere more so than in the mind of the great actor David Garrick (1717–79), of whom his friend Dr Johnson said, 'The theatre made Garrick rich and he made the theatre respectable.'

Garrick was so obsessed by Shakespeare that in 1756 he built a temple to the great playwright at Hampton, west of London on the Thames, and close to the former home of the great Augustan poet Alexander Pope. After a recent restoration, this remarkable building is now open to the public, but only on Sundays. The temple looks rather like a small version of the Pantheon at Rome – it is a single room with a dome and a four-column Ionic entrance that faces east. Garrick built it to house his collection of Shakespearian artefacts. The temple is open on Sundays but only in the summer, from March to October.

A chair made for Garrick by Hogarth from a mulberry tree said to have grown in the garden of Shakespeare's house in Stratford was sold after Garrick's death and is now in the Folger Shakespeare Library in Washington D.C., while a statue of Shakespeare by Louis-François Roubiliac (who used Garrick as a model) is now in the British Museum. But what is really so intriguing about this temple by the Thames is that, to make sure he could get to it easily each day from his house nearby, Garrick had to dig a tunnel under a roadway. He used to learn his lines by walking up and down the tunnel where nothing could distract him – 'not even birdsong', as he put it – and the temple was kept for 'contemplation' and as a place where Garrick could write to his huge number of friends. Indeed, Garrick was such a prolific writer that the postman would call especially each day to collect a sack of letters.

SIMPSON'S CHOP HOUSE

1757

The old City's courts and alleyways contained – at least until the Second World War – many early merchant's houses and mansions divided up into small offices or converted into pubs. Better still, many of these alleyways contained what was once a city institution – the chop house. This was a cheap restaurant where city workers could eat their lunch.

Most were characterised by a room divided by wood panels into small snug areas where friends could meet undisturbed. Most of the courts and alleyways, the mansions and chop houses were swept away by bombs and redevelopment; those courts that remained became sanitised with bright new bars and tall office blocks replacing the old subdivided houses, but against all the odds at least one chop house has survived in its original court. Simpson's can be found in Ball Court right in the heart of the old City. Founded in 1757, it still has its panelled divided snuggeries.

NUMBERS GAME

1759

Many of London's houses conceal remarkable interiors, but none more so than No. 29 Piccadilly. This classical house might easily be taken for a twentieth-century attempt at Georgian architecture; in fact, it is one of the earliest remaining buildings in what was once one of London's most fashionable streets.

Piccadilly started to be developed from around 1661, when the land at what is now the eastern end of the street was given to Henry Jermyn (1604–84), 1st earl of St Albans and adviser to Charles II. The role of the earl is recognised today in the name of nearby Jermyn Street. Inns and shops were first built overlooking the park and down towards Buckingham Palace (Buckingham House, as it then was), while at the other end were the grand mansions of the rich. Piccadilly had been known as Portugal Street in honour of Charles II's queen, Catherine of Braganza (1638–1735), but when Robert Baker, a tailor, made his fortune selling lace collars known as picadils, he bought a big house at the western end of Portugal Street, which became known as Piccadilly Hall.

The name stuck and soon the whole street became known as Piccadilly and poor Catherine was forgotten. Nothing survives from the earliest period of development except parts of St James's Church and the core of Burlington House, now home to the Royal Academy. Coventry House was built between 1759 and 1762 for Sir Henry Hunloke, a Derbyshire baronet, on the site of an old pub called the Greyhound Inn. By the mid-1760s, the 6th Earl of Coventry had bought a lease on the house and it was he who employed the great architect of the day, Robert Adam, to alter and decorate the interior in the latest fashion. Astonishingly, much of his work still survives to this day, despite numerous (and not always sympathetic) owners.

Coventry sold the house to Napoleon III's future ambassador, Comte de Flahault de la Bellarderie, in 1848. Then, from 1868–1978, the house became the St James's Club. Since then, the house has had a number of commercial owners, but still Adam's work survives. If you want to see it, however, you will have to visit Sir John Soane's Museum in Lincoln's Inn Fields where, astonishingly, there are 56 exquisite drawings of the interior of Coventry House, and many of the rooms they depict are still there just as Adam and his men left them.

There is one final remarkable thing about Coventry House: it was originally No. 29 Piccadilly when built, but is now No. 106. The number has changed simply because so many magnificent houses in the street were demolished in Victorian times and, later, because the number of houses and shops decreased dramatically. One tragic loss is Devonshire House (the wine cellar became the booking office for Green Park Station), but the magnificent gates from this long-lost mansion can still be seen almost opposite Coventry House and now form part of the Green Park railings.

MOZART IN PIMLICO

1765

The connection between Mozart and London might not be immediately obvious, but legend has it that the young Mozart composed his first ever symphony in a small house in London. Incredibly, that little house is still there, and is one of a short row of early eighteenth-century houses built in what is now Pimlico.

When the row was built it was a stone's throw from one of the great social and entertainment centres of eighteenth-century London, Ranelagh Gardens. The gardens are named after Ranelagh House, a mansion that once stood on the site. It had been owned by the 1st Earl of Ranelagh (1641–1712), treasurer of Wren's great retirement home for ex-servicemen, the Chelsea Hospital. The late seventeenth-century house was almost adjacent to the hospital, and its grounds ran down to the river. The gardens are still there but they no longer reach the river – they have been separated from the Thames by the Embankment that was built at the end of the nineteenth century.

Ranelagh Gardens was conceived and opened by Thomas Robinson, who owned the Theatre Royal in Drury Lane. He had a keen sense of what the public wanted and knew that a spectacular feature would attract people upriver from London and also away from his great competitor, the famous gardens at Vauxhall, which had been established almost a century earlier.

For the centrepiece of his new attraction, Robinson came up with the idea of what he called the rotunda. With a diameter of 120ft (36.6m), a central chimney, fireplaces and grand boxes lining tier upon tier of galleries, the rococo rotunda was one of the great attractions of eighteenth-century London. Much of the entertainment offered in the rotunda was music, and it was here in 1765 (although some sources suggest he played here on 29 June 1764) that the nine-year-old Mozart astonished the assembled crowd with his brilliance at the keyboard.

The rotunda is long gone – the RHS Chelsea Flower Show takes place on much the same ground – but the little house where Mozart stayed before walking across to the gardens to give that dazzling concert is still there, in Ebury Street. Remarkably, almost all the other houses in the row have been lived in by famous inhabitants – including the great garden designer and writer Vita Sackville-West.

LEAPFROGGING BISHOP

1767

Edward Hervey (1730–1803) joined the church because he wanted a job that paid well but involved almost no work. His brother was the Bishop of London, so when Edward was offered the bishopric of Boyne in Ireland, he took it. Some years later in 1763 he was offered the even more lucrative bishopric of Derry, so he took that too. Weary of Ireland, he soon moved to London and employed someone else (on a pittance) to carry out his ecclesiastical duties.

Hervey was very eccentric and he had a particular love for the game of leapfrog, which he insisted the junior clergy join in. While in London in 1767, he tried to persuade the Bishop of Southwark to introduce a rule that all future Bishops should have to play leapfrog at least once a year. His fellow bishop was appalled at the suggestion and refused. Hervey was indignant and left Britain for several years to travel in style and at great expense across Europe.

HAWKSMOOR'S CONDUIT

1770

One of the strangest historical remains in London must be the Standard Reservoir Conduit House at Greenwich. When one thinks of the great architect Nicholas Hawksmoor (c.1661–1736), who was responsible for such magnificent churches as Christ Church Spitalfields, one forgets that in addition to his church work Hawksmoor was Clerk of the Works at Greenwich Hospital in south London from 1698–1735.

He almost certainly built the conduit house that survives in Greenwich Park. It was built above a reservoir designed to supply the Royal Hospital for Seamen at Greenwich with fresh water. This was one of the earliest attempts to bring water by pipe (or conduit) to London.

The building is in remarkably good condition, but even more extraordinary is the 656ft (200m) stretch of brick conduit tunnel that survives under the conduit house leading down towards the old hospital, which is now the National Maritime Museum. The fine brown bricks and classical style of the conduit house belie its purely functional origins. The walls include beautifully carved, eighteenth-century graffiti, including the name 'M. Pinfold' and the date 1770.

FOR WHOM THE
BELLS TOLL

1774

The church of St Sepulchre-without-Newgate isn't as strange as its name may sound to modern ears; the 'without' refers to its position just beyond – i.e. outside – the old city gate (Newgate). Named after the Holy Sepulchre in Jerusalem, what we see today is largely a late-Georgian remodelling of a much older church which, like so many of London's churches, was destroyed in the Great Fire of 1666. The Victorians couldn't keep their hands off the church either, so a great deal that is not Georgian is late nineteenth century.

Apart from its name, what makes St Sepulchre fascinating is that it still retains the old handbell that was rung outside the cell holding the condemned at the old Newgate Prison. On execution days the bell would be rung and the condemned led out to a cart that would then carry him or her along the Tyburn Road (now High Holborn and Oxford Street) via St Giles near Seven Dials and then finally to Tyburn (now Marble Arch), where the execution by hanging would take place.

But these were not always gruesome occasions. Particularly unpopular prisoners were, it is true, pelted with dead cats and rotten vegetables, but there were also prisoners who were heroes, and they would be cheered all the way from Newgate Prison to Tyburn. In fact, so popular were some of the condemned that the authorities had to marshal a large contingent of soldiers to guard the prison carts or tumbrels, in case the mob attacked them in an attempt to rescue the prisoner. As one wag put it: 'The heroes of the day were often on good terms with the mob, and jokes were exchanged between the men who were going to be hanged and the men who deserved to be.'

The old bell now sits in a glass case, but no doubt the vicar will allow you to hear its ghostly sound if you ask him. Another curious custom observed at St Sepulchre's was the presentation of a nosegay to every criminal on his way to execution at Tyburn. No doubt the practice had its origin in some kindly feeling for the poor unfortunates who were so soon to bid farewell to life. One of the last who received a nosegay from the steps of St Sepulchre's was John Rann, alias 'Sixteen String Jack', who was hanged in 1774 for robbing the Rev. Dr Bell of his watch and 18 pence in coins, in Gunnersbury Lane, on the road to Brentford. Sixteen String Jack wore the flowers in his buttonhole as he rode to the gallows.

This was witnessed by the antiquarian John Thomas Smith, who describes the scene in his book documenting the life of the sculptor Joseph Nollekens, *Nollekens and his Times*: 'I remember well, when I was in my eighth year, Mr Nollekens calling at my father's house, in Great Portland Street, and taking us to Oxford Street, to see the notorious Jack Rann, commonly called Sixteenstring Jack, go to Tyburn to be hanged. The criminal was dressed in a pea-green coat, with an immense nosegay in the button-hole, which had been presented to him at St Sepulchre's steps; and his nankeen small-clothes, we were told, were tied at each knee with sixteen strings. After he had passed, and Mr Nollekens was leading me home by the hand, I recollect his stooping down to me and observing, in a low tone of voice, "Tom, now, my little man, if my father-in-law, Mr Justice Welch, had been high constable, we could have walked by the side of the cart all the way to Tyburn."'

THE SOMERSET DEADHOUSE

1776

Somerset House – designed by Sir William Chambers and built in 1776 – may not be as interesting as the Tudor palace it replaced, but it does have some intriguing aspects. This vast palace was built as a statement – there had long been complaints that London did not have a huge official building created in the most up-to-date architectural style of the time.

The new Somerset House was meant to remedy this, with its long Neo-classical Strand frontage, and even more impressive river frontage. Until the Embankment was built, the Thames flowed under the walls of Somerset House and the river terrace, painted by Canaletto among others, was one of the great sights of London.

But less well known is the curiously named Somerset Deadhouse. This is a long passageway that allows daylight to reach the windows of the basement rooms of the palace. The narrow passageway is hugely popular with makers of period films – most recently *Sherlock Holmes* starring Robert Downey Jr. But here and there along these passageways are tombstones that are believed to date from the time of the earlier palace, and almost certainly from the chapel built by Charles II for his French (and therefore Catholic) wife Queen Henrietta Maria. The chapel and its burial ground were demolished along with the whole Tudor palace, but some of the tombstones were repositioned discreetly within the new palace, presumably at the express request of someone in the royal family with Catholic sympathies.

Placing the tombs in the Deadhouse would have been discreet enough to avoid arousing the anger of the London population, which by the end of the eighteenth century was going through a fiercely anti-Catholic phase.

ATTENTION, COLUMNS!

1783

The National Gallery was built on the site of the Royal Mews – the place where horses and birds were 'mewed up' (confined). It is justly famous though as when it was built the architects were furious that they had to build along a very narrow strip of land – the exact strip formerly occupied by the king's stables. The gallery also includes the famous pepper pots on the roof – these are fake versions of the ventilation grills that existed on the old stables – and a very curious set of columns at the front. Most people assume these columns were designed and built for the gallery, which was completed in 1838 to the designs of William Wilkins, also responsible for a number of Cambridge University colleges. Much altered and extended over the years, the gallery remains a classical masterpiece, and the columns at the front are a key part of this, but they were not built for the gallery at all.

They formerly stood at the front of Carlton House at the bottom of Regent Street facing up towards Piccadilly Circus. Carlton House was built for the Prince Regent at enormous public expense and completed in 1783, but no sooner was it finished than he decided it wasn't good enough for him and he had it demolished. The columns from the front of the building were saved and carried along Pall Mall and installed at the front of the new National Gallery.

One other amusing story about the gallery is that at various times there have been plans to charge people for looking at the pictures. When this was tried in the 1980s, it caused a furore and almost resulted in the gallery losing half its pictures. What the trustees hadn't realised was that many of the pictures had been donated to the gallery on the express understanding that the public would always be able to see them free of charge. This small but vital clause could not be overturned, which is why, uniquely in Europe, the British National Gallery does not charge an entrance fee.

NAKED KING
1788

The fact that George III was considered to be mad for much of his reign was certainly a disaster for the monarchy and a personal tragedy for him, but it had some remarkably positive consequences, not least of which was a transformation in attitudes generally to madness.

Before George was afflicted, those deemed 'insane' were usually very badly treated. Traditional 'cures' included starvation, whipping and confinement in the dark, and were based on the medieval idea that madness was caused by possession by the devil.

Thus, it followed that if the mad were whipped and burned and beaten, the evil spirit within them would become increasingly uncomfortable and leave the poor patient alone. But when the King of England went mad, people soon realised that a monarch could not be whipped and confined to a damp, dark cellar, even if it was suspected that he might be possessed by demons. Instead, kinder measures were tried (although the king did have to put up with some indignities), and these kinder measures eventually became the basis for the modern treatments of mental illness.

But, as it turns out, George III wasn't, strictly speaking, mad at all. His symptoms were actually the result of porphyria, a rare genetic condition in which a chemical known as porphyry builds up in the brain because of a lack of certain other chemicals designed to break it down. In some cases – and the king's was one of these – the disease leads to periods of anxiety and severe hallucinations. It was these hallucinations that the king experienced that led to some extraordinary antics. The first of these prolonged episodes began in 1788.

At Kew Gardens, for example, he once chased the writer Frances Burney across the lawns with a team of horrified courtiers in hot pursuit, and on many other occasions the king would run naked through his court. In a moment of supreme folly, which may or may not have been connected to his mental afflictions, in 1800 George III decided to build a vast gothic house at Kew. The original estimate for the house was £40,000, a colossal sum in the eighteenth century, but by the time building stopped (and the house was still unfinished), the bill had risen to a staggering £500,000.

Parliament simply refused to allow the king any more money and the project was abandoned. What was worse was that the house, or as much of it as had already been built, was then demolished.

George III also has a peculiar connection with Australia that originates from his passion for merino sheep. He had them imported from Spain so they could run around the gardens at Kew – some say this was just so he could run around after them! Eventually they became the basis for the whole Australian sheep economy as all Australian merino sheep are descended from the small group of animals that once roamed the grounds of Kew.

A BRIDGE TOO FAR

1791

The curiously named Thousand Pound Pond is one of the delights of the grounds of Kenwood House in north London. No one knows for sure where the pond gets this curious name, but the best guess is that it comes from the early 1920s, when preservationists were desperately trying to save as much of this part of Hampstead Heath as possible from the developers. They persuaded the owner of Kenwood House, Lord Mansfield, to sell some 32 acres (13ha), including the woodland and lakes we see today, but Mansfield demanded a staggering £1,000 per acre (0.4ha). The pond covers about 1 acre of the land, so by my calculations the Thousand Pound Pond seems about right.

The pond itself was formed in 1767–68 and rebuilt in 1791, and its creation was part of that huge eighteenth-century enthusiasm for landscaping. But the oddest thing about the lake is the beautiful bridge that has long been admired by visitors. Even today when people come to admire the woodland walks and visit the beautiful house with its priceless collection of pictures, they inevitably think to complete their visit by crossing the white bridge at the end of the pond. Visitors soon realise, however, that this is completely impossible. The bridge is a sham and is just a few inches in width. It was created when the pond was made simply to provide an attractive view and is virtually two-dimensional, a cardboard (or timber) cutout.

RIVER POLICE MUSEUM

1798

The United Kingdom has a reputation for eccentricity and, among a host of eccentric institutions, top of the list must be our museums: there are fan museums, lawnmower museums and even fishing-reel museums. But in London you would have to go a long way to find a more eccentric museum than the River Police Museum at Wapping Police Station.

This splendid building is still a working police station but in the old carpenter's workshop you will find a unique collection of uniforms, truncheons and even cutlasses; cutlasses (a short sword with a slightly curved blade) were issued to the river police for some years after they were founded in 1798.

The river police were established because of the enormous amount of contraband that came up the River Thames and the fact that it was easy for criminals to escape by boat to the southern shore if they were being pursued. The smugglers' trick was to leave a boat tied up at the bottom of one of the numerous flights of stairs that led down to the water, much as a criminal might have a getaway car today.

For the first century and more after they were established, the river police rowed themselves up and down the river and, since they were not always as hardy as the criminal rowers, it was not always easy to make arrests. Around 1900 they finally acquired paraffin-engine boats and later the diesel-powered launches of today.

RABBIT-PROOF FENCE

c.1800

Many people forget that until well into the 1960s London's Royal Parks still had a population of rabbits, and signs in Kensington Gardens still explain that it was forbidden to annoy the sheep. The rabbits that inhabited the parks may well have been descendants of rabbits introduced and carefully protected in the Middle Ages.

At this time, no grand menu was complete without a dish that included rabbit, which was eaten only by the very wealthy. But by the eighteenth century, rabbits had spread far and wide and because everyone could now eat them, the rich lost interest. Indeed, rabbits had become pests and the carefully protected warrens where they had once been allowed to breed unhindered became things of the past.

However, despite this change in status, some rabbits did survive in the Royal Parks, and proof that they were once there can be seen in the design of the eighteenth-century railings that run along the backs of the old houses in Birdcage Walk opposite St James's Park.

Look carefully and you will see that the 6ft (1.8m) railings have shorter spikes, around 2ft (0.6m) high, between their main spikes. Their purpose was to reduce the gap between the main spikes so that rabbits couldn't pass through them. Just because there were rabbits in St James's Park, the gardeners in the grand houses around it did not want their carefully tended plants to be eaten by starving bunnies!

POWDER MAGAZINE

1805

Buildings used to store gunpowder were historically known as magazines. They were usually, though by no means always, situated in remote areas because of the danger of explosions – modern nitro-powders are far less likely to be accidentally ignited, but 'black powder', as it was known, is extremely volatile. Astonishingly, one of these buildings still exists in central London.

This is the Hyde Park magazine, situated on the north side of the beautiful stone bridge across the Serpentine built by John Rennie (1761–1821). The distinctive Greek Revival-style building, with its columned portico, was completed in 1805 and there is no doubt that one of the main reasons it was built here was that Hyde Park had long been (and still remains) a place of popular protest. If a popular rising had to be suppressed using firearms then they might as well be stored in Hyde Park, and that was the justification for building the magazine here.

Powder magazines of this type were built with very little metal – typically even the floorboards would be positioned using wooden dowels rather than nails in order to reduce the risk of an explosion. Remarkably, the Hyde Park magazine was still owned and run (as a general storeroom) well into the 1960s.

STARED OUT BY THE REGENT

1805

Bedford Square in Bloomsbury was built in the 1780s as an upper-class enclave. In its early years, it certainly attracted the wealthy and well-born, if not always the aristocracy, and it is a good example of a tendency that occurred across London in earlier centuries.

As London expanded, the rich would often move out to enjoy the cleaner, leafier surroundings, and their once-great mansions frequently began a long period of decline. The great houses of Piccadilly, for example, were built to allow an escape from the squalor of the old City of London, but as tradespeople, shops and other businesses moved here, so the grandees moved further away. Their old houses would then be sub-divided and let initially to the less well-off, and then later to the poor and then the very poor. As a result, the buildings deteriorated and were usually demolished. The rich wanted new houses in areas where the light was good and there was space – and no poor people.

Bedford Square represented one stage in this process. When it was first built, there was still open country to the north and so it attracted the city's wealthiest inhabitants, one of whom was the 1st Earl of Eldon (1751–1838), who served as Lord Chancellor. Eldon had only recently moved into the square when he began to be pestered by the Prince Regent, who wanted him to give one of his friends a job that paid very well but demanded almost no work at all;

the friend was Joseph Jekyll and the job title was Master in Chancery.

Eldon disliked the Prince Regent intensely and had been avoiding him because he was hoping to offer the lucrative job in question elsewhere, but the Prince Regent got the better of him.

He turned up one morning at Eldon's house in Bedford Square in 1805 and was told by the butler that his lordship was ill and could not see anyone, even a prince. Despite his huge bulk (he was enormously fat by this time), the Prince Regent brushed past the servant and lumbered up the stairs before opening the door of every room on the first floor. He eventually discovered Eldon in one of the bedrooms and sat down opposite him. Wasting no time, he told Eldon that he wanted the job for his friend. Eldon refused and the Prince Regent said, 'In that case, I must tell you that you will never see your wife again.' For a second Eldon must have thought the prince intended to murder him – or, indeed, his wife. However, remaining calm, he replied, 'What on earth do you mean?'

The prince replied: 'Well, I am not moving from this seat until you agree to my terms.' Silence fell and Eldon decided that the prince must be bluffing. He said nothing and stayed in his bed. He got up and went to the lavatory and returned to bed. The prince's eyes followed him everywhere. Several hours later the prince was still there and still staring at Eldon who, by this time, was feeling deeply disturbed. Eldon finally gave in and agreed to give the coveted post to the prince's friend.

FRENCH FOR BOLLARDS

1805

Bollards are a commonplace in London and surely many people have noticed how the old cast-iron examples are shaped rather like cannon. Indeed, it was usual among London children playing in the street in Victorian times to refer to the bollards as cannon. The bizarre truth is that the first bollards installed in London were not made to look like cannon – they actually *were* cannon.

The reason for this is that so many French cannon were captured after the Battle of Trafalgar in 1805 that the government, rather than waste them, decided they would be a useful way of preventing the iron-shod wheels of London's tens of thousands of carts and cabs from damaging kerbs and the corners of buildings. The captured cannon were driven into the ground and the idea became so popular and proved so successful that, as they corroded or wore out, replicas were made in iron, but were still designed to look exactly like the original upended cannon. Today, their tough plastic descendants are still designed to look rather like cannon.

Astonishingly, if you wander the South Bank near the Globe Theatre, you can still see a few of the original French cannon still upright and doing the job for which they were not really designed more than 200 years ago!

TOMB RAIDER

1809

The Victorians, it has often been said, were obsessed by death. This was partly because during Victorian times the influence of the monarch was considerable. When the Queen's Consort Prince Albert died from typhoid in 1861, the queen went into mourning for the rest of her life – and what a long life it was. The queen wore black every day and gradually so did her subjects, as this was a time when the public slavishly aped the monarchy and criticism of the royal family was almost unthinkable. This stood in stark contrast to the Regency period in the early years of the nineteenth century, when the Prince Regent was regularly pilloried in the newspapers and by cartoonists such as Gillray and Rowlandson.

Queen Victoria's obsession with death led to a whole new style of architecture. The gloom of gothic, which had been exciting and new in the 1830s when Parliament was rebuilt in a gothic style, gradually became a dead style, leaden and gloomy and weighing heavily on social and civic life. This was reflected as much if not more than anywhere else in Victorian cemeteries. When London parish churches were finally forbidden to bury any more bodies in their overcrowded graveyards, large municipal cemeteries opened in the suburbs, and the extra space encouraged those who were half in love with death to build ever bigger and more elaborate monuments to those who had died.

Kensal Green Cemetery, which was very fashionable after it opened in 1833, has some wonderfully elaborate gothic tombs; likewise the Egyptian tombs of Highgate Cemetery. But perhaps the strangest tomb of all is hidden away in a small churchyard on the edge of London.

In Pinner Parish Church – the thirteenth-century church of John the Baptist – there is a giant stone tomb that looks rather like an arrowhead. There is an arch that runs through the base of the structure to create this shape, which has elaborate ironwork and the words 'I bide my time' engraved on its surface. Perhaps the oddest thing about the monument, apart from its sheer size, is that protruding from either side of the vertical stone face are what look like the two ends of a coffin! The tomb was built by the horticultural writer John Claudius Loudon for his father, William, who died in 1809. John's mother Agnes died in 1841 and was also buried here.

The story behind the tomb is at least as curious as the tomb itself. Apparently William and Agnes Loudon had inherited a large amount of money through a family will, but that money could only come to them if they were buried above ground. The elaborate tomb was thus, in part at least, a way to keep the money in the family! John Loudon was a fascinating character who wrote several important horticultural books and was an important influence on the development of that most characteristic London feature, the garden square. He also invented the curved iron glazing bar that made Paxton's Crystal Palace possible. An opium addict, he was in the process of designing Southampton Cemetery when he died penniless in London in 1843. He is buried in Kensal Green Cemetery, in a tomb that is considerably less elaborate than the one he built for his parents.

DEAD TEETH

1815

A Piccadilly dentist placed the following advertisement in *The Times* in around 1790. 'Wanted: human front teeth. Apply to Mr Wogffendale, 21 Dover Street, Piccadilly.' Dentistry had become something of an obsession in late eighteenth-century London, and doctors and dentists were baffled by the fact that the rich tended to have far worse teeth than their poorer cousins.

The simple answer – that sugar rots teeth – was not yet known, but it was a simple fact that sugar consumption increased in exact proportion to an individual's wealth. Thus, in this respect, the poor were luckier than the rich in that they at least kept their teeth longer!

The near universality of bad teeth explains why in portraits of the time it is almost unheard of to find the sitter smiling. It was not that they did not want to appear cheerful, it was simply that they did not want to display their appalling teeth. One of the Founding Fathers of the United States, Benjamin Franklin (1706–90), was an early recipient of the latest in London dentistry – during his residence in the city he famously had a set of wooden false teeth made.

However, by 1800, dentists began to replace lost teeth with the teeth of the dead. This may seem rather gruesome to us today, but in the early nineteenth century, when sophisticated materials such as porcelain were not available, using real teeth seemed the obvious answer and a great improvement upon wooden teeth. Thus began a huge trade in teeth harvested from the dead.

After the Battle of Waterloo in 1815, the trade in human teeth reached its zenith and dozens of poor Londoners set off for what is now Belgium to dig up the hastily buried dead on the battlefield that made the Duke of Wellington famous. The great thing about these dead soldiers was that most were young and from poor backgrounds, so their teeth were usually in reasonably good condition. As a result, thousands of rich Londoners ended up wearing the teeth of the war dead, and what's more, there is no evidence that the rich even questioned where their new teeth had come from!

The teeth were cut down and fitted to base plates of ivory, which were hinged. Small springs were added so that when the wearer opened his or her mouth the dentures opened too. These crudely made dentures must have been very uncomfortable and they almost certainly fell out now and then, but they were perhaps better than no teeth at all. As late as the 1850s human teeth were still widely available in London and elsewhere.

UGLY QUEENS
1815

The arrival of William of Orange in England and the exile of King James II famously solved the problem of Catholics inheriting the British crown, enshrined in the Act of Settlement of 1701. William was reasonably popular with the British, as was Anne, his sister-in-law, who reigned following William's death in 1702 following a fall from his horse. However, there was always a sense among the traditionally irreverent British that foreign princes were not to be taken too seriously. And the habit of mocking the monarchy became a key feature of much of British life from the arrival of George I after Anne's death in 1714.

George had only one real claim to the throne – he was Anne's closest living Protestant relative. George was mocked by the British public because his English was poor and he was constantly going home to Germany. Many people thought he was illiterate and stupid, but this had more to do with his rather wooden public persona than any genuine lack of intelligence. But if George was mocked, so too were his son and grandson, George II and George III. By the time of George IV, the British had largely forgotten the German origins of their royal family, and they were so used to their monarchs behaving immorally with a succession of mistresses that they didn't worry about that either. But when George IV attempted to divorce his wife, Caroline of Brunswick, the public was outraged.

It was said that George, then Prince of Wales, had only married Caroline because she was rich and his gambling debts were huge, but in those pre-photographic days George had to agree to marry Caroline without ever actually having met her. George had seen paintings of his bride-to-be, but court painters of the time were employed to flatter their sitters rather than strive for accuracy, so when George met Caroline for the first time, in 1795, he was horrified. She was so ugly he wanted to call the marriage off, but of course this was impossible. It was the start of a terrible relationship that made George immensely unpopular. If he had remained married to Caroline but enjoyed the favours of the aforementioned mistresses, few would have complained – after all, that was what monarchs traditionally did.

Caroline's role was to provide a male heir, but she even failed to do that. Her daughter was born in 1796, by which time George was refusing even to see her. George eventually became king in 1820 and Caroline died, still as his queen, in 1821. He had tried to divorce her soon after becoming king, but this was extremely difficult, even for a monarch. George tried to find proof of adultery in order to justify the separation – absurd and hypocritical, since his own adulterous relationships had long been the talk of the town. But George had another even more insurmountable difficulty – prior to marrying Caroline, he had already married someone else! He is the only bigamist king in British history (although his first marriage, to Maria Fitzherbert, was judged invalid on the grounds that she was a Roman Catholic and the king had not given permission for it to go ahead).

George failed in his attempts to divorce Caroline, partly because she was so popular with the British public, who took her side largely because they hated her husband. She was excluded from his coronation, and instead stood outside with her supporters who jeered her husband; it had all the makings of a farce. Caroline fell ill the same day and died three weeks later, thus solving the problem.

It is this highly volatile relationship that has produced one of London's strangest tales. George so hated Caroline that he insisted that the house she had lived in following their estrangement, on Blackheath, south London, should be razed to the ground. Caroline went abroad in 1813, and two years later the demolition went ahead. It is said George intended that no trace of the house should remain, but in the 1990s a tiny part of the house was rediscovered. If you want to see where Caroline once bathed at Montague House you still can – the sunken bath with its short flight of steps can be seen in Greenwich Park.

OLD STONE TO NEW BUILDING

1820

Various bits of Old London Bridge found a new life when the ancient structure was demolished towards the end of the eighteenth century. One or two of the old stone alcove seats went to Victoria Park and the timber piles made at least one piece of furniture (a fine chair now owned by the Fishmongers' Company), but many people have wondered what happened to the thousands of tons of fine-cut stone that was carted away over the several years it took to pull down the old bridge.

The truth is that almost none of the stone was wasted. Much of it was of the highest quality and as it had already been cut and shaped it was eagerly snapped up by various builders of the day. The bulk of it was bought by Edward Harman, who owned the Ingress Estate in what is still officially Kent, but is actually now part of London's huge urban sprawl, near the Bluewater Shopping Centre.

In the thirteenth century, the manor of Greenhithe was the site of Britain's only abbey devoted to Dominican sisters. During the Dissolution of the Monasteries, which took place between 1536 and 1541, the estate was sold and the abbess put a curse on Henry VIII, which many believe explains why the son and heir he longed for died so young and without children of his own. Some believe the curse is handed down to all those who own the estate, and that it will remain in place until it is returned to the Dominican sisters.

By the mid-eighteenth century, having passed through the hands of several owners, the estate was bought by Viscount Duncannon and, like all the previous owners, he did not manage to keep it in the family for long. By 1820, James Harmer, a London alderman, was in possession, and started to build the house we see today, the fifth on the site. In the spirit of the times he opted for a deliberately old-fashioned look, designing the house in a way that echoes a Tudor gothic style.

The new house was called Ingress Abbey – a deliberate nod to the long-vanished Dominican sisters. It overlooked the Thames and was much admired by visitors. But what makes the house genuinely unusual is that the stone from which the whole house is made was once part of Old London Bridge. Harmer's architect Charles Moreing bought a huge amount of the reclaimed stone, which had lain unused in a stonemason's yard for decades. So, if you want to see Old London Bridge – as famous in its day as the Rialto in Venice or the Charles Bridge in Prague – you can at least get some sense of it by visiting this beautiful house in Greenhithe.

BUILT ON WATER
1824

The church of St John's Waterloo is unique among London churches in that it is largely held up by muddy water. This may make it sound as if this is a church that should be avoided if you wish to escape having tons of rubble collapsing on your head, but paradoxically the muddy water has made the church one of the most stable in London.

To find out why it was built on water we need to go back to the early nineteenth century, when London was expanding rapidly as the Industrial Revolution drew in hundreds of thousands of people from rural areas. Parliament, always far more concerned with the spiritual nourishment of its citizens than their physical welfare, decided that more churches were needed for this increased population, so the Commissioners for New Buildings voted £64,000 (an enormous sum at the time) for a new church to be built on the road leading to Waterloo Bridge.

The decision to build St John's was taken in 1822 and the building was completed in 1824. Curiously, and despite the growing passion for the gothic style, the architect chosen for the new church was a Greek scholar, the splendidly named Francis Octavius Bedford (1784–1858). Not surprisingly, he insisted on building a Greek Revival church, and no sooner had it opened than it was subject to a torrent of abuse from modernisers who insisted it should have been built in the newly fashionable gothic style.

The church may have been unfashionable from the outset, but the architect had the sense to consult the great engineer John Rennie the Younger (1794–1874) before starting work. The problem was that this part of London sat on deep marsh; however far down the engineers dug they found only oozing mud and then water. In those pre-concrete days a solid raft could not be built easily as it would for a tower block or other structure today, so Rennie suggested a solution that the Romans and other much earlier builders had relied on: he proposed driving long oak piles – in essence sharpened tree trunks – deep into the mud below where the church walls were to be built.

It was known at the time that oak used in this way could easily last thousands of years: a well-preserved oak pile from the Roman river embankment had recently been discovered and is now preserved in the entrance porch of the church of St Magnus the Martyr at the north end of London Bridge. But it was still a risk. Rennie's confidence, however, inspired Bedford and his plan worked brilliantly. Even a direct hit by a bomb in 1940 only damaged the rood and interior. The walls, on their springy base, bounced back and were used in the restoration of the church, whereas other church walls on solid foundations had to be demolished after bomb damage.

In the 1970s and 1980s, the tunnel for the Jubilee Line was built beneath and close by the church, and the ground, waterlogged for thousands of years, began to dry out. The church quickly became unstable, and had the drying process continued it would have collapsed. The solution was to restore the watery base that, combined with ancient oak, had preserved the church for so long. So, millions of gallons of river water were pumped back into and around the church foundations. The result once again is a remarkably sound building, which should last for a thousand years.

BETTER THAN THE QUEEN'S HOUSE

1825

In 1825, building began on a mansion just a few hundred yards from Buckingham Palace. This mansion – once the most expensive private house in London – was designed for the Duke of York, the second son of George III, and during construction was known as York House. The architect Robert Smirke was first to be employed on the project, but he was quickly sacked in favour of a friend of the Duke of York's mistress, the Duchess of Rutland. She insisted that Benjamin Wyatt be given the job. Wyatt designed the exterior we see today, and this is in fact the last grand mansion in London to be designed in the Neo-classical style.

Gothic had already become the current trend, so it is remarkable that York House was designed in what was widely seen at the time as a rather outdated style. But the strange history of the house continued when the Duke died long before the house was completed, and it was sold unfinished to the second Marquess of Stafford, and renamed Stafford House. The interior, for which Smirke was re-employed along with Wyatt and others, was so elaborate and magnificent that it wasn't finished until 1840. Indeed, this house was so grand that when Queen Victoria came to dinner she stood in the great staircase hall and said to her host, 'I come from my house to your palace.' Whether this was meant as a slightly sarcastic remark or a compliment is difficult to say!

In the early twentieth century, as aristocratic families ran out of money and gradually sold many of their huge London houses, Stafford House was bought by the industrialist and soap-maker Lord Leverhulme. He renamed it Lancaster House after his favourite county and then a year later he gave the house to the nation. From 1924 until the mid-1940s, the house became the London Museum, but it is now used as government offices. It is open to the public only occasionally.

ARM'S LENGTH

1826

Few people under the age of 60 now remember in any detail the old coinage system that was replaced in the early 1970s, when Britain moved over to the decimal system. The old system was a nightmare for visitors used to coinage being based on multiples of ten: there were 20 shillings to the pound and each shilling could be split into 12 pennies. There were crown coins (five shillings), half-crown coins (worth two shillings and sixpence) and even threepenny pieces. Many other equally strange coins, including the farthing (a quarter of a penny), only went out of circulation in the 1950s.

Equally as strange as the monetary system was the old system of measurement, and in many parts of London this ancient system is still reflected in the width and height of houses, as well as the layout of squares and parks. It is astonishing that, until well into the twentieth century, houses were built using the old imperial system, which was based on the ninth-century furlong – from old English *furh* (meaning 'furrow') and *lang* (meaning 'long'). This was the measurement of an agricultural strip.

As a result, most Victorian and Georgian buildings in London are constructed on the basis of a system of measurement that pre-dates the Norman conquest. For the uninitiated, a furlong is 660ft (201m) long; 1 acre (0.4ha) is 1 furlong long and 1 chain (66ft/20.1m) wide. Smaller divisions (which would have been used for house plots) were known as the rod, pole and perch: 4 rods were equal to 1 chain and 1 chain in London was used to measure four house fronts. Builders' rules were based on the fathom, which was the distance between two outstretched arms.

When modern metric measurement systems began to be used in London, the old unity was broken, but many houses remain to show us how the influence of the Saxons on London buildings lasted more than a thousand years. A magnificent example of the old measurement system in practice can be seen in Belgrave Square, where building started in 1826. The square was laid out to measure precisely 10 chains by 10 chains. As it has never been altered since it was completed in the first half of the nineteenth century, it still baffles modern surveyors!

QUEEN IN A CELLAR

1831

One of the greatest architectural losses in London was the destruction in the early nineteenth century of the church of St Dunstan-in-the-West. The church that existed at that time dated back to the tenth and eleventh centuries, and it escaped the Great Fire of 1666 through the quick thinking of the Dean of Westminster. In the middle of the night he woke dozens of schoolboys, formed them into a chain and instructed them to throw buckets of water over the flames as they approached the church along Fleet Street where the fire, though still burning, was not raging quite as fiercely as it was at the other end of the street closer to the City proper.

The nineteenth-century obsession with updating and rebuilding London's churches destroyed this remarkable structure, and the architect John Shaw (and his son, also named John) was employed to rebuild the church in 1831. During rebuilding a remarkable discovery was made: a statue of Queen Elizabeth I was found buried nearby. Today this is the only statue of the queen in London and the only likeness known to have been carved during her lifetime. It probably stood originally in a niche in nearby Ludgate, the entrance to the City from the west.

Other treasures in the church include numerous monuments saved from the earlier building. The world-famous clock on the wall outside, high above Fleet Street dates back to the 1670s.

A PIECE OF OLD LONDON BRIDGE

1831

Old London Bridge, which was demolished in 1831, would have been one of the wonders of the world had it survived until today. Over the 600 years of its existence the bridge survived fires, the collapse of several of the arches on which it was built, and an attack by Wat Tyler during the Peasants' Revolt. At the height of its fame, the bridge supported around 150 shops, a palace and numerous houses. There was a gatehouse at either end, and high above the turrets of the southern gatehouse were the long pikes on which traitors' heads were stuck until they rotted away.

But, of course, the bridge had its drawbacks; the roadway between the houses and shops was very narrow, which impeded the traffic; the bridge's 19 irregularly shaped arches so impeded the river water that, upstream, the Thames regularly froze in winter and the rush of water in summer through the arches was highly dangerous. Only the most experienced boatman would attempt to 'shoot the bridge'. Few lamented the final destruction of this marvel, but one or two sentimentalists wanted to keep some memory of a structure that had epitomised London for so long, so at least one of the old stone pedestrian alcoves that once lined the bridge was carefully removed to Victoria Park in east London, where to this day it serves as a shelter for pedestrians. Its beautifully cut stone arch and bench reminds us that London Bridge was once the pride of the city.

PRISON FARE

1834

London's ancient prisons with their harsh regimes are
no longer, but for those prepared to look carefully in odd
places, traces remain. One wall of Marshalsea Prison in
Southwark, south London, can still be seen, for example.

This prison became famous after Charles Dickens made
it the focus of his novel *Little Dorrit*. Dickens knew it well,
as it was the place where his own father was imprisoned
for debt. But among London's least-known and strangest
prisons was Tothill Fields Bridewell. It was also known
at various times as Tothill Fields Prison, Westminster
Bridewell and the Westminster House of Correction.

Built in what were then the slums of Westminster, the
prison began life in 1618. It was named after Henry VIII's
palace on the banks of the River Fleet. Originally one of
the king's favourite residences, the palace was handed over
to the City of London Corporation by Henry's son Edward
VI, and it became a prison, or, more precisely, a house of
correction, but the name Bridewell became synonymous
with prisons generally. Tothill Bridewell was unique in that
prisoners were very rarely whipped or punished violently by
any other means. Instead, the prison imposed an absolute
rule of silence on its inmates. Anyone who broke the rule
had their food ration withdrawn for a day or two.

In 1834, Tothill prison was rebuilt on a new site where
Westminster Cathedral now stands, at the opposite end of

Victoria Street from Westminster Abbey. The rest of the site was covered over with red-brick mansion blocks, many of which survive to this day. The prison foundations were so extensive that they were used to provide a foundation for the massive cathedral that now stands on the site, but Westminster Council did decide to keep one part of the prison intact. The prison's stone gateway was moved to Little Sanctuary behind the Middlesex Guildhall and just across the road from Westminster Abbey, where it can be seen, though it is easily missed, to this day.

MPs' SNUFFBOX

c.1835

The House of Commons has long been famous for its rather eccentric practices. Until recently, for example, any MP wishing to interrupt a certain kind of debate had to don a top hat before rising to his or her feet to speak.

The building in which MPs do their work is perhaps equally eccentric. Because it was designed by the great – and obsessive – high priests of gothic, Augustus Pugin and Charles Barry, it was bound to have a very real medieval flavour. This was achieved in part at least by including sword rests here and there in various rooms, even though by the time the Commons was built in the 1830s, swords had long been an anachronism. The building's designers also forgot that any building by the side of a river is likely to subside – which is why the Palace of Westminster (as the two Houses of Parliament are jointly known) sinks an inch or so into the mud each year.

So eccentric is the design of the building that it includes vast numbers of tiny hidden voids under the floors, between the walls and behind the wainscot (lower section of panelling). The result is that there is no accurate and complete map of the underlying structure of the building, which in turn means that every attempt to get rid of the half a million or more mice that infest the palace has failed.

Many visitors wonder why, after wartime damage, the House of Commons was deliberately built with too few seats for all the MPs. The answer reveals the extraordinary power of one man: Winston Churchill. It is impossible today to imagine that one man, even if he happened to be prime minister, could insist that Parliament be deliberately made too small and get away with it. But this is exactly what Churchill did. He knew that it is rare for the house ever to be full, since attendance at debates is rarely compulsory for MPs. Given that there would usually only be a relatively small number of MPs in the house at any one time, he thought a small chamber would ensure that it always looked relatively busy. Churchill also wanted to retain the intimacy of the medieval St Stephen's Chapel, which had previously been the Commons Chamber.

WORLD'S LONGEST ROPE

1837

Camden Market in north London is one of the most popular shopping destinations in the capital. Packed with stalls selling clothing – everything from the retro to the bizarre – the market is especially popular as many of its buildings were once associated with horses and barge traffic on the canal that runs through the site. Indeed, the whole of the market area has a wonderful historic feel to it.

It is rambling and ramshackle, rather like a medieval souk, and many of the stalls have been set up in the old stables where the bargees' horses were once housed. Beneath Camden Market, things are even more exciting, for here there are miles of underground caverns and storerooms. Indeed, they stretch for such a distance that it has never been considered safe to open them to the public.

There is also a large subterranean hall, constructed in 1837 for the London and Birmingham Railway – a truly remarkable survivor. It once housed a huge steam engine and cablewinding mechanism designed to haul steam trains up the hill from Euston Station in the days when the steep incline (1 in 85) was still too great for the engines then in use. Despite the skill of the great engineer Isambard Kingdom Brunel, who built the railway here, nothing could be done to reduce the steepness of the climb north out of the station. The ingenious solution was this remarkable winding engine.

The stairs down to the wheelhouse still exist and the wheelhouse itself is 115ft (35m) long, 23ft (7m) high and 14¾ft (4.5m) wide – all constructed of magnificent brickwork and shaped stone. An operator waited for a signal from Euston Station a mile or so down the hill, he would set the coal-driven steam engine going and the train would be hauled up the hill at around 15mph (24.1km/h) until the incline was sufficiently gentle to allow the carriages to be coupled to a locomotive that would continue its journey under its own steam. The rope used was the longest piece of unspliced rope ever created, at almost 4,000 yards (3,658m) long. It was 7in (17.8cm) in circumference and weighed more than 11 tons! Double engines (two locomotives coupled together at the front of the carriages) were used from 1847 to pull trains up the hill and the winding house fell into disuse, its machinery demolished. But the fact that the hall was so long forgotten helped its survival and, thankfully, it is now a listed, and therefore protected, structure.

SQUARE RULES

1840

One of the biggest changes in London over the past 200 or so years is the disappearance of private roads and private squares. Until well into the twentieth century, many streets had railings and gates across them to prevent street traders, hawkers and vagrants from gaining access.

A typical street might even employ a watchman in a little house at either end to lock the gates at night and keep watch. The cost to the residents must have been considerable, but such was the perceived nuisance of the great unwashed that hundreds of these heavily restricted streets and squares existed. Almost all have now vanished. Ely Place in Holborn is an exception, and here the railings that kept out the undesirables remain.

Some private streets and squares also had some odd rules, and few were stranger than those applying to Bedford Square in Bloomsbury. Here the watchmen would make careful enquiries of anyone who wanted to enter the square. The idea was not just to exclude beggars, street musicians and hawkers; it had far more to do with ensuring only gentlemen and ladies were allowed in. It is hard to imagine today just how easy it once was to tell by a person's dress and demeanour the class to which he or she belonged. Great efforts were made by the idle rich to dress as carefully and elaborately as they could, partly to display their finery (and by implication their wealth), and partly to indicate to all and sundry that they belonged to a certain class.

The poor and the middle classes had neither the time nor the money to dress in the manner of the rich, because in the days before elastic and zips dressing up involved elaborate preparation by a team of servants. At Bedford Square, only those dressed in a certain manner were admitted. Even the respectable poor had no chance of entering, but there was a problem: tradesmen had to be let into the square or the residents would starve and be without coal and candles.

A solution was reached: the residents and watchmen of the square let it be known that only the owners of the coal merchants, the grocers, butchers and so on would be admitted. This was a problem too, because hard-pressed shopkeepers employed boys and young men to deliver their goods but not, it seems, in Bedford Square. If they wanted to sell here in the square, they had to deliver their parcels in person. At the time this was regarded as an excellent piece of one-upmanship and other streets and squares that tried to ape their betters thought they would copy the Bedford Square rule.

Today the railings and watchmen have gone, but Bedford Square remains one of the finest and least-altered Georgian squares in London.

In the 1970s, a concealed entrance was discovered in the cellar of one of the houses and inside more than 200 bottles of wine dating back to 1840 were found. They were sold for a small fortune at auction, and even the earliest was perfectly drinkable.

GRAVEDIGGER'S COTTAGE

c.1840

The Drury Lane area of London now looks rather grand, but in earlier centuries it was notorious for crime and prostitution. It was part of a large area stretching from what was the notorious region of Seven Dials just north of Covent Garden, to the even more notorious slums surrounding Wych Street that lay to the south of Drury Lane, running down towards the river.

The whole of Wych Street and the surrounding area was destroyed in the early twentieth century in order to build what is now Southampton Row and the Aldwych. The medieval houses that the current monolithic buildings replaced would have been the envy of Europe had they survived, for they all pre-dated the Great Fire of London of 1666. The street pattern here too was medieval, but the problem was that the area had gone down in the world. Formerly grand houses were subdivided over the centuries as the wealthier moved out to the suburbs of Park Lane and north towards Oxford Street. The poor swarmed into Wych Street and those surrounding it and landlords spent nothing on repairs.

It is not surprising then that the area was one ripe for redevelopment, but one house in the area has survived – the famous so-called Old Curiosity Shop on Portsmouth Street. However, there is also a far less well-known and equally curious survivor on Drury Lane itself. Here, surrounded by blocks of late-Victorian flats to which the poor of Wych Street were moved, is a tiny park. In fact, this was one of London's most notorious graveyards, where bodies were deposited just below the surface and bodysnatchers, who stole the recently deceased and sold them to medical students, were a constant problem.

Historically Londoners had the right to be buried in the graveyard of their parish church, but as the city grew this became increasingly difficult, and by the middle of the nineteenth century, burials involved pressing new bodies in flimsy coffins into already over-filled graves. Eventually things got so bad that gravediggers were forced to jump on the coffins to push them down beneath the surface, and they were then covered with just a few inches of soil. The result was appallingly unhygienic and no doubt contributed to high infant mortality rates in poor families: one in three babies died before they were a year old. At last, in 1851, London's small burial grounds were closed by an Act of Parliament. As the years passed, the graveyards were emptied of their bones and the headstones were often stacked around the edges of the new open space. At Drury Lane, all signs of the site's former purpose have disappeared – or at least that's how it seems. In fact, two red-brick gothic buildings from the mid-nineteenth century, still stand flanking the entrance to the garden: one was the gravedigger's cottage, the other the former mortuary where bodies were kept before burial.

POET'S STOLEN FURNITURE

1846

Consecrated in 1817, St Marylebone Parish Church – its portico based on the Pantheon in Rome – replaced a small brick church built in 1740. The old church became a chapel of ease and survived until 1949 when it was demolished.

But what makes St Marylebone Church so interesting is that it was here that one of the greatest love affairs of the nineteenth century reached its celebrated conclusion.

The story of Robert Browning's elopement with Elizabeth Barrett is too well-known to repeat at length, but the essence of the story is that the great poet fell in love with a girl who appears to have spent much of her life before meeting Browning resting on a sofa in the way that delicate, middle-class women were supposed to at that time. Her father by all accounts made great efforts to convince his daughter that she was too ill for any of the usual pleasures of life, let alone marriage, but when she and Browning met they fell in love and, knowing how opposed her father would be to the match, the two married in secret – at St Marylebone Church – and eloped to Italy in 1846.

The story became one of the great love stories of the Victorian era, and for many years the church preserved much of Browning's furniture in a room kept apart for the purpose.

Today, all that remains is the church register recording their marriage, as over the years the furniture has all been stolen. The room, bare and functional, is now used for meetings.

DOG-LICK REPLICA

1847

One of the strangest sights in south London is the statue of a dog licking out a pot that stands on a replica cast-iron bracket at the top of a post at the corner of Union Street and Blackfriars Road, just near Southwark Tube station. The golden-brown metal dog with its head half in a black pot is a reminder of a famous sign that once stood on a bracket outside J.W. Cunningham's shop at 196 Blackfriars Road. This splendid shop was in business from the late eighteenth century until 1931, when the town planners decided to demolish most of the buildings.

The original handmade brass and timber dog and pot was preserved and is now in the Southwark Museum. It, and the replica that now stands on its post, is a reminder not just of a famous sign, but also of the fact that London businesses were famous for erecting eccentric or elaborate signs to draw attention to their businesses. A good sign would soon be the talk of the town and would draw customers from far and wide. Clockmakers would put clocks outside their businesses – Morgan's, a famous clock and watchmaker's shop in Acton, west London, went one better and put a huge clock around 6ft (1.8m) square above its door. The shop itself was only about 12ft (3.7m) wide! Wooden signs showing a Native American chief were popular outside tobacconists' shops (the idea that they smoked peace pipes seems to have been the connection), and large wooden fish might be hoisted above the doors of fishmongers and fishing tackle shops.

The dog and pot in Southwark is also famous because it was seen every night by a young Charles Dickens as he walked home from the boot-blacking factory just off the Strand. He mentions the sign at length in a letter to his first biographer, John Forster, in 1847. Dickens would have been saddened at the destruction of almost every building he would have known along that walk, but he might also have been surprised that the golden dog he knew is now a curious shade of brown!

NIGHTINGALE'S OWL

c.1850

Florence Nightingale is deservedly famous as the founder of modern nursing. Born into a privileged, wealthy home, she had to fight to be allowed to work at all in an age when to do nothing was considered the only proper occupation for a middle-class woman. She more than anyone in the nineteenth century understood the need for hygiene and clean air in hospitals. She became so influential that when St Thomas's Hospital moved to Lambeth in the mid-nineteenth century she was largely responsible for the courtyard design of the wards, a design that ensured maximum light and air. Today, one of London's most unusual museums is dedicated to her life and work, and located in the hospital where so many of her ideas are embodied. Here you can also see Florence's best friend preserved forever by a taxidermist.

Her best friend was actually a Little Owl called Athena. She had discovered Athena as an abandoned chick in Athens (hence the name) and, using her nursing skills, kept the tiny bird alive when it was on the brink of death. It thrived, became an adult bird and refused to leave her side for the rest of its life. Wherever and whenever Florence travelled, Athena went with her in a specially enlarged pocket in her dress. When Athena died she was sent to the taxidermist and so looks today just as she looked in life.

The museum is also home to the slate on which Florence Nightingale learned to write as a child. A statue of the famous nurse can be seen at St Thomas's too, but this is a copy of the original that was stolen in 1970. The statue would not have been valuable, and it was so famous that any thief trying to sell it would have been immediately arrested, so its disappearance remains a mystery. One theory is that an admirer of Nightingale simply had to have it, and it remains in his or her collection but well out of sight of the public.

THE LAST OF DEVIL'S ACRE

c.1850

Modern visitors are often astonished to discover that what was one of the worst, most insanitary and overcrowded areas of London in the mid-nineteenth century is now one of the most expensive and fashionable.

The area around Westminster Abbey and the House of Commons was once known as Devil's Acre. The name was a reflection of the endless narrow streets of small, badly built and disease-ridden houses that ran from Westminster down towards Victoria Station in one direction and towards Vauxhall Bridge in the other.

A clue to the former poverty of this area can be found in the vast numbers of flats that now exist in the Tachbrook and Peabody housing estates, just a stone's throw from Parliament Square, which are still inhabited in many cases by the descendants of those who lived in Westminster's slums before they were cleared in the 1930s and 1940s.

However, a few of the small houses that were once typical of this area do survive. A short walk from Parliament Square leads you to Gayfere Street. Here you can see three very small, third-rate houses of a kind that once ran in every direction. Smartened up and lived in by the super-rich today, they are nonetheless a reminder of what this part of London once looked like. Another similar example can be found in Old Queen Street, a narrow alleyway that runs off Storey's Gate near Westminster Abbey. Here two tiny, late seventeenth-century houses survive, crammed in and overshadowed by later buildings. And if you visit Strutton Ground, about half a mile (0.8km) down Victoria Street from Parliament Square, you will see a few more examples of the sort of houses that once existed here.

TAXING TIMES

1851

The British government has a reputation going back centuries for trying to find ingenious new ways to tax the public. The trick today is to find a tax that it is difficult to avoid. Of course taxes – as someone famously once said – are for little people, and wealthy members of government have themselves always been as keen as any super-rich private citizen to find ways to avoid tax. In previous centuries, wool was taxed along with salt. At various times there have been attempts to tax wallpaper, fireplaces and even bricks. Taxing things people simply can't do without was also popular – which is why alcohol has always been so heavily taxed.

It also explains why smuggling became such a huge industry on the south coast of England in the seventeenth and eighteenth centuries. Recent tax dodges by large firms and wealthy individuals who have simply moved their cash overseas (while claiming to be good citizens) were perhaps inevitable. But taxing land and property rather than other forms of wealth has always been a better idea, because it's not so easy to move your land and your property out of the country. However, tax avoidance was not the reason for the introduction of a window tax in England in 1696.

As the title of the act makes clear, the new tax was to grant 'to His Majesty several Rates or Duties upon Houses for making good the Deficiency of the clipped Money'. 'Clipped money' refers to the habit ordinary citizens had of biting small pieces off the edges of valuable coins – which made sense when coins were still actually made of gold and silver. At this time, income tax did not exist – in fact, income tax in the form in which we know it today did not exist until as recently as the mid-1840s. The window tax was simply based on how many windows you had. There were exemptions for the poor and for those rooms deemed to be dairies or pantries, however, which caused a sudden increase in the number of rooms labelled 'dairy' or 'cheese room'.

Until the modern habit of completely rebuilding house interiors began in the 1980s and 1990s, it was still possible to see the old painted dairy sign above rooms in old houses. But, despite attempts to avoid the tax in this way, those owning houses with anything between ten and 20 windows were charged a flat rate of four shillings (about £25 in today's money); if your house had more than 20 windows you had to pay eight shillings (£50). For houses with fewer than nine windows, a flat rate of two shillings was charged, but of course no sooner was the tax introduced than people began to try to avoid it, which is why we still see many early eighteenth-century houses with many of their windows bricked up.

The tax lasted until 1850, when a particularly dark and gloomy winter made people feel that the window tax was really a tax on light and air. It was finally repealed in 1851, but of course no one wanted to pay the cost of removing the bricks from those long-bricked-up windows, which is why they have lasted to this day.

MAGGS' GHOST

1853

London is full of ghosts. Most theatres more than a century old are said to have ghosts – usually bad-tempered actors who did not succeed in their careers – and many churches are the same: theirs are usually women who died of a broken heart, or disgruntled vicars with a grudge against their former parishioners.

But it is rare for an ordinary shop to have a well-attested ghost, which is why Maggs Bros Ltd., the antiquarian bookseller's in Mayfair, is so unusual. Founded in 1853, Maggs is one of the oldest and most prestigious antiquarian booksellers in the world. Their shop, housed in a beautiful Georgian building in Berkeley Square, attracts collectors from all over the world, and at Maggs it would not be difficult to spend £100,000 on a single book. They will sell you an individual book but they much prefer, as they say themselves, to build relationships with collectors who buy regularly. This means the shop can be rather intimidating if you are not already a millionaire bibliophile.

No. 50 Berkeley Square has been Maggs' home since the middle of the twentieth century, but in the nineteenth century this house was known as the most haunted in London, to the extent that, for many years, it remained empty because no tenant could be found to take on the lease. In his 1907 book *Haunted Houses*, Charles Harper records that during a period when the house was untenanted, in the 1850s, lights were often seen flashing in the upstairs windows and faint screams could be heard by passers-by. The whole west side of Berkeley Square came to be avoided by superstitious souls who preferred to cross by the east side and avoid the risk of hearing unearthly groans.

The legend of this haunted house seems to stem from an early tenant, who kept his mad and extremely violent brother locked in the attic, feeding him twice a day through a hatch in the door. Visitors to Maggs as recently as 2005 have reported seeing odd shadows flitting through the building or sensing a presence. One visitor even had his glasses knocked off as he walked up the stairs. Understandably Maggs make no mention of these strange goings-on in its literature and advertisements ...

DINING WITH THE EARL

1857

The eccentric Francis Egerton, 8th Earl of Bridgewater (1756–1829), never married. He rarely left his estate, and as he grew older became ever more slovenly and bizarre in his habits. He made a servant follow him constantly carrying a large box of snuff, he insisted on wearing a different pair of shoes for every day of the year, and he never threw anything away.

As a result of his hoarding, his large London house groaned under the weight of old boxes and trunks, umbrellas, chests filled with old curtains, suits and rugs, discarded wrapping papers, broken-down chairs and tables, countless pictures, books, papers and piles of assorted domestic refuse.

But, among all his eccentricities, there was one that distinguished Bridgewater from every other dotty aristocrat in the land: his love for his dogs. He owned over a dozen and he treated them as if they were his children. Some were strays he'd taken a fancy to while walking the streets; others were purebred hounds and gundogs; still others were tiny lapdogs. All were allowed to sleep with the Earl and to eat with him. Indeed, every evening he would have his huge dining room table laid with the best linen and silver cutlery, and each of the dogs would sit in a chair in its allotted place. The dogs were expected to dress for dinner, and the only time the Earl shouted was if they jumped down before the meal was finished.

Several times a year the Earl travelled by train from London to his home in the country. Normally one or two dogs would accompany him, but on one extraordinary occasion all of them came along. Bridgewater paid for 15 first-class tickets for the dogs and took over two whole compartments.

To make sure no stranger tried to enter either of the two compartments – this was in the days when compartments could not be reserved – he sent his servants on ahead to the station to bar the entrances to the carriages in advance of the Earl and his party of dogs. During the journey, each dog took a seat in one or other of the compartments and the Earl wandered between the two, making sure his favourites were enjoying themselves. Other passengers looking for a vacant seat found the blinds of the compartments drawn and the Earl's 'No Entry' signs posted on the windows.

On one never-to-be-forgotten journey, Bridgewater fell asleep and on waking went to check on the dogs. He found to his horror that six entirely new dogs – 'I'd never met them before,' he declared later – had somehow joined his favourites. Unused to strange dogs, the Earl's normally well-behaved hounds were barking and jumping and biting each other. It took the Earl and his servants some time to restore order and to reject the interlopers.

Bridgewater was so outraged by what he described as a 'serious violation of his dignity' that he threatened the railway company with legal action, and it was only a visit from one of the directors that smoothed the troubled waters. Though the railway company officials privately agreed the Earl was a damned nuisance, he was a good customer with powerful friends – so the doggy train journeys continued and, as far as history records, without further mishap.

MULTIPLE GEORGES

1857

Pratt's Club is based in a narrow, terraced house in Park Place, just off St James's Street, and it is surely one of the oddest private members' clubs in the world.

It reputedly has around 600 members, yet has room for only 14 at any one time around the single tiny dining table in the basement. The club, too, was not founded by a group of aristocrats or members of the same trade. Indeed, the house where the club is based was once the home of William Nathaniel Pratt, a servant employed as steward by the Duke of Beaufort. The club began when Beaufort and a few friends dropped in on the steward one evening in the 1850s and had so much fun they kept coming back. By 1857, the club existed formally and began to take new members. But, despite the growth in membership, they couldn't bear to move and find new, bigger premises.

Even today, therefore, the club still only has two rooms – the aforementioned dining room and a small sitting room. There is a billiard room, too, but it is apparently only used to store members' coats! The club is marvellously old-fashioned – there is no central heating and no lift, despite the advanced average age of the members and the 100 and more steps between the basement and the top of the house.

But Pratt's greatest claim to fame is the bizarre tradition concerning its staff. All the male staff for as long as anyone can remember have been called George, and if you apply for a job at Pratt's today you still have to agree – as one of the conditions of service – to be called George.

The tradition is believed to have started because Pratt's members were so habitually drunk that they could never remember the real names of their servants and all resorted to 'George' to save confusion. A difficulty arose when the club employed its first waitress. The problem was quickly solved when they decided to call her Georgina.

DOG POLICE OFFICER

1857

Bow Street near Covent Garden gets its name from the fact
that the long, curving street originally resembled a bow.
Laid out in the seventeenth century, the street was later
extended north and south, which altered its shape. Bow
Street is of course best known for the Bow Street Runners,
often said to be the first modern organised police force
in the world. Less well known is that the runners' ranks
included a dog.

Until recently anyone who passed the old Bow Street
Police Station would have noticed two doors: one for the
police and prisoners, the other a long-disused, iron-gated
doorway.

It was at this gateway, in 1857, that an old, starved and
generally sickly-looking dog tried to make a home, only to be
driven away again and again by order of the superintendent.
Subsisting on the charity of passers-by and of the men of
F Division, whose headquarters were at Bow Street, the
dog soon became hearty and strong and, having always
returned to his chosen spot, now resisted all further
attempts at removal.

As the various sections of police left the office to relieve
the men on duty, the dog always followed them, and as soon
as the last man's place was filled up he would return to the
doorway. As a result, the men became so interested in the
dog that, on their encouragement, he took up his quarters

inside the station, was named 'Charlie', and was even considered to be a member of the police force. Received into the office, where, according to the police regulations, he had no right to be, Charlie, also known as the White Sergeant, was placed on the official dining list and at the Christmas dinner was allowed to sit at the table.

On state occasions, when the greater part of the division was required, a sergeant's armband was buckled around his neck, and he seemed to be very proud of this decoration. On one occasion, at a Victoria Cross presentation in Hyde Park, more than 500 policemen were present. However, on this particular day Charlie had accidentally been shut up in a room at the station.

As soon as he was set free he ran to the park, worked his way through the immense crowd that had gathered and took his position at the head of his own division. With the sergeant's armband in place, Charlie sat as stiff and erect as an old soldier in front of the long line of constables. As she passed, Queen Victoria honoured him with a smile.

At a quarter to six every morning, the first shift of men paraded in the yard at the Bow Street Police Station. Charlie was always present, marching up and down the front of the line with all the importance of a drill sergeant. On such occasions he was always accompanied by the only four-footed companion he was known to have – Jeanie, the police office cat, who, with a bell tinkling on her brass collar, trotted at his side. With the parade over, Charlie led the men in their march around the area covered by Bow Street Police Station.

At least once each week he set out on a tour of the district, waiting for a while with any policeman who might be a favourite. When, however, parade time drew near, no inducement would prolong his walk, and off he bounded, always reaching Bow Street in time to drill the men. When the ten o'clock night relief went out, Charlie, after duly doing the rounds, returned to eat with the men who had been relieved from their shift; but as soon as the meal was over he went out on patrol once again, returning to the station in time for the midnight parade of men.

There were only two exceptions to his punctuality. Once, Charlie watched for some days by the deathbed of an old constable to whom he was much attached, and on the other occasion he had been severely mauled and nearly poisoned by some of the thieves of Seven Dials, to whom he was well known, and whose schemes he had often assisted in defeating.

But Charlie's greatest feat was yet to come. Early one morning, a constable, while passing through New Church Court, a narrow lane off the Strand, was knocked down by two men. Charlie, who was a short distance behind, ran across the Strand to the police station in Somerset House and, seizing the sergeant on duty there by the tails of his greatcoat, led him to the constable's assistance. The constable was found to have been severely wounded and without Charlie's intervention might have been killed outright.

When he grew old and unable to do his rounds, Charlie spent much of his time at the kitchen fire. He died of old age at the police station, in front of that fire, in 1869.

LEANING BEN

1859

The tower most people call Big Ben is perhaps the most famous symbol of London, far more evocative of the capital than the London Eye, or even the red bus. Opened in 1859, Big Ben was previously known as the Clock Tower, before being renamed Elizabeth Tower in honour of Queen Elizabeth II's Diamond Jubilee in 2012. During Victorian times journalists referred to the tower as St Stephen's Tower, as any news related to the House of Commons was referred to as coming from 'St Stephen's'. In Wales the name persists and Parliament is known as 'San Steffan'. These names, however, have always been ignored to some extent, as the clock tower is really only ever referred to as Big Ben, which is actually the name of its biggest bell.

Despite its fame, the 315ft (96m) high tower has a rather sinister history. Indeed, the difficulties of designing it (not to mention much of the rest of the Palace of Westminster) drove architect Augustus Pugin (1812–52) to madness and death. Already overworked by the need to create thousands of designs for other parts of the Palace of Westminster, Pugin, the arch-priest of the new gothic style, was exhausted by the time he finished the drawings for the tower and he never recovered.

Another bizarre feature of the tower is that only UK residents may visit the interior. This can only be done through one's

MP and there is a long waiting list. There is also no lift, so the tower can only be climbed via more than 300 stone steps.

One final curious fact about the Elizabeth Tower is that it leans more than 9in (22.9cm) to the north-west and, depending on the weather and temperature, it moves slowly back and forth as the year progresses and the weather gets gradually warmer and then colder!

BLACK ROD'S BOYS

1860

The office of Black Rod, or (to give it its full name) the Gentleman Usher of the Black Rod, is well known; at the State Opening of Parliament he walks from the House of Lords to the House of Commons and has the door slammed in his face for his pains. The door is slammed in Black Rod's face as a reminder that Charles I was thrown out of the chamber in 1642.

Having knocked on the door three times with his ebony (black) rod, he is allowed to enter in order to summon the Commons to the Lords' chamber to hear the Queen's Speech. But Black Rod has other duties – he can arrest any lord who misbehaves (very rare) and he is also responsible for the buildings and security of the Palace of Westminster (as the Houses of Lords and Commons are collectively known).

Black Rod has one final and rather odd duty. Each year he is obliged to organise a tea party for the children attending nearby Westminster School. The tea party is held, appropriately enough, in Black Rod's Garden, where a small pavilion was built in 1860.

THE LAST
OSTLER'S HOUSE

1860

The role of the ostler is one that vanished with the coming of the motor car. Before motorised transport, thousands of men up and down the country spent their lives in this ancient profession. Their job was to attend to their master's horses. That meant that when a gentleman returned to his house on horseback (or in his carriage), it was their job to take his horse to the stable, feed it and settle it for the night. Ostlers were also employed by the thousands of inns across the country that existed to serve the needs of travellers and their horses. London still has one remnant of this ancient trade and it is overlooked by almost everyone – the ostler's hut in Lincoln's Inn Fields.

This is said to be the smallest listed building in London. It is certainly one of the most charming, with its red-brick and stone detailing. For more than 40 years after it was built in 1860, the hut was where the ostler attached to Lincoln's Inn looked after the horses of the lawyers and their visitors. The hut fell out of use early in the twentieth century and was quietly forgotten as horses gradually disappeared from London's streets.

FROM PANORAMA
TO CHURCH

1868

Just north of Leicester Square in Leicester Place is an odd little church that most people hardly glance at twice. Certainly from the outside the building is not especially noteworthy, but in fact it is a survivor from the 1860s when the French Marist Brothers bought the old Burford's Panorama that had been there for more than half a century.

The Marists (actually 'the Society of Mary') were founded in the nineteenth century and given the responsibility of taking Christianity to Africa and elsewhere. The panorama they purchased in London was an early form of cinema, which showed a painted scene that was slowly turned by a system of wheels and cogs, giving spectators gathered in the centre the impression that they were watching a great procession. But the Marists needed a place for the French community in London to worship and so they reconstructed the panorama to create a church that still offers services to this day. But what is little known is that the round church follows the exact shape of the panorama and may even incorporate parts of the earlier structure. The architect of the new church, the largely forgotten Louis-Auguste Boileau, used a revolutionary material for his new church – cast iron.

The Church of Notre Dame de France, as it is known, is also remarkable for its extraordinary murals by Jean Cocteau (1889–1963). Cocteau is best known as a film-maker, but towards the end of his life he came to London especially to paint the murals in this church. The pictures are vaguely post-impressionist in style, and show scenes from the life of Christ, as well as a self-portrait of Cocteau. There is also a splendid mosaic by the Russian artist Boris Anrep (1883–1969) who was a close friend of the Bloomsbury Group and completed a better-known mosaic at the nearby National Gallery using his Bloomsbury friends as models.

HOPPING SOUTH
OF THE RIVER
1868

One of London's less well-known and yet historical buildings is the old Hop Exchange in Southwark. Built in 1868, it was the last of its kind, following the destruction of the Coal Exchange in the 1960s and the old Stock Exchange after the Second World War. Hops had become big business after their introduction to England from Holland in about 1500. Such was the importance of the new plant that it inspired the following rhyme:

Hops, carp, bays and beer
Came into England, all in a year.

Ale had previously been the national drink in England. It was made with barley and lacked the bitter taste imparted to modern beers by hops. Ale was drunk by everyone because water was too dangerous – the process of boiling the water for ale made it safer to drink, and even children drank large quantities of ale safely because it was much weaker in terms of alcohol than modern beers. Despite misgivings about the new flavour provided by hops – one commentator described the hop plant as 'a pernicious and wicked weed' – the new bite it imparted to beer quickly became popular, and hop fields, or hop gardens as they were known, were planted increasingly across Kent. The harvest was then shipped by boat and later by train and road to London.

Those who traded in hops needed somewhere to conduct the business of buying and selling and so, in 1860, plans were drawn up to build a hop exchange with a naturally lit trading floor. To this end designer R.H. Moore created the spectacular frontage we see today at 24 Southwark Street. But the really spectacular bit of the building is hidden inside – the exchange hall is a mass of glorious gothic windows, wrought-iron balustrades and tiled floors lit from a soaring glass roof. It has now been converted into offices and events space.

GREATHEAD'S TUNNEL

1869

There is a long history of digging tunnels under the River Thames, and one reason for this is that London is built on clay, which is a relatively stable material for digging. The first Thames tunnel was dug by Cornish miners between Wapping and Rotherhithe in the eighteenth century, but after water broke through on several occasions it was abandoned.

The first successful tunnel was built by a team that included Isambard Kingdom Brunel and his father Marc. It was dug between 1825 and 1841, again between Wapping and Rotherhithe. It succeeded after the invention, by the Brunels and an engineer called Thomas Cochrane, of a tunnel shield that allowed the tunnel to be dug inch by inch and then immediately shored up behind the cutting face. Though it cost far more than it should have, the Wapping tunnel was hugely popular and a tourist attraction in its day. Even Queen Victoria paid a visit. The tunnel still exists but is now used by the London Overground.

Another, altogether stranger tunnel was dug between the Tower of London and the south side of the river, and this largely forgotten tunnel explains a curious brick-built, circular building at Tower Hill. This is all that remains above ground of Mr Greathead's tunnel, known as Tower Subway, on which work began in 1869.

James Greathead (1844–96) was a brilliant civil engineer who helped perfect the kind of tunnelling shield used by the Brunels for their earlier tunnel. This was in essence a tunnelling machine that supported the tunnel from collapse even as it was dug. Greathead's innovations are still the basis for modern tunnelling equipment – but the tunnel he built at an astonishingly low cost is now used to carry mains water across the river, and all that remains of his efforts above ground is the small, round entrance building.

BLOW-UP BRIDGE
1874

The pillars of Blow-Up Bridge, which crosses the Regent's Canal near London Zoo, are the first thing the passing walker (or canal barge passenger) notices. Immensely thick and made from cast iron, they seem almost too robust for the narrow brick bridge they support. These pillars, however, are the only remnants of the first bridge that crossed the canal at this point – a bridge, moreover, that was blown up in one of the biggest explosions the capital has ever experienced. To understand how the accident happened we have to remember that the pretty tree-lined canal we see today is a relatively recent phenomenon.

For almost 150 years after they were dug, England's canals were grimy industrial corridors through the landscape. Their sole purpose was to move heavy goods from one industrial part of the country to another. They did this very cheaply and very efficiently – so much so that there are plans to return them, in a limited way, to their original use. The Grand Union and Regent's Park canals were among the most important of these watery highways. Massive loads could be moved at low cost on barges pulled by one or two horses. Once the horses got the barge moving, its momentum would keep it going, so canals were cut from the Thames up to Birmingham, Manchester and beyond.

It might seem a slow process but it was cheap, with the bargees living with their families in tiny rooms at one end of their long narrowboats and the rest of the boat piled high with coal, steel or pottery. Then, on a fateful day in 1874, a barge loaded to the gunnels with gunpowder passed under what was then known as Macclesfield Bridge. No one knows precisely what ignited the powder, but the resulting explosion was heard across the whole of London. 'It was like a deep thump that moved the ground,' recalled someone living in the notorious potteries district of North Kensington, some 4 miles (6.4km) away. The explosion destroyed the bridge, and of course hardly a scrap of the boat and its inhabitants could later be found, but the massive cast-iron pillars were recovered – one or two from the canal and at least one from a field more than 100 yards away. The pillars were reused in the bridge we see today, and if you look carefully you will see that they were put back the wrong way around. The deepest grooves cut by the ropes that had pulled the barges are now on the towpath side of the pillars, rather than on the canal side where they should be.

PET DRINKS

1875

Burying one's pet with an elaborate headstone and the sort of inscription one would normally expect to see on a human memorial was, to a large extent, invented by the Victorians. Famously obsessed by death, the Victorians turned funerals into an art form, with elaborately plumed black horses pulling engraved glass hearses draped in mourning black.

This fascination with death was matched by an increase in sentimentality when it came to dogs, cats, parrots and budgerigars. Thus pet cemeteries began to appear across London – a famous one exists tucked away on the north side of Kensington Gardens – but the love of pets also led to a curious feature of many parks. Until recently, both Green Park and St James's Park were home to lampposts featuring tiny stone drinking troughs at the bottom, with minuscule lead pipes leading into them. Placed there in the latter part of the nineteenth century, the idea was that passing dogs (and perhaps cats) would always be able to have a drink. Presumably the rabbits that lived in Kensington Gardens until the mid-1960s were also able to enjoy a refreshing sip at these quirky watering holes.

BONE-TASTING WATER

1876

We are so used to having water on tap that it is difficult to recall a time when houses and squares, courtyards and alleyways across London relied on water that had to be pumped by hand from wells dug deep into the London clay. Until recently it was claimed that at least one of the Inns of Court still privately pumped its water up from the River Fleet, but even if working pumps are now a thing of the past, some wonderful examples remain.

Shoreditch Churchyard contains a fine example, as does St Paul's Cathedral, and one or two suburban churchyards now boast pumps moved from their original positions in the streets and kept for sentimental reasons. A fine pump exists by the front wall of St Mary's Church in Acton.

Possibly the grandest of these memorials to drinking water is the tall, ornate, cast-iron water pump in Bedford Row, just off Holborn. Charles Dickens lodged near this area and it is easy to imagine he would have helped himself to water here. But the oddest must be the pump attached to the wall of Staple Inn, just to the south of Chancery Lane Underground Station. The original pump that stood here has long vanished, and the one we see now is a replacement – but it dates to a time long after there was any need for hand pumps and no one seems to have a clue why it was fixed here. It remains one of those unexplained mysteries.

The oldest pump still in its original position is probably the blue-painted example at Cornhill just outside the Royal Exchange. This pump is inscribed with the following words: 'On this spot a well was first made and a House of Correction built thereon by Henry Wallis Mayor of London in the year 1282.' The pump is dated 1799.

But perhaps the most interesting specimen of all is the Aldgate Pump, so called because it stands at the junction of Aldgate and Fenchurch Street. It was moved here from Aldgate Pump Court, where a pump had stood from at least the reign of King John. The court was demolished to make way for Fenchurch Street Station but until 1876, the pump drew its water from an underground stream. It was channelled into the mains system in 1876 after people started to notice that the water had a distinctly chalky flavour. The cause was quickly found: the underground stream ran through a number of plague pits and graveyards on its way to Aldgate and so densely were the skeletons packed in these graveyards that the stream was picking up large amounts of calcium from the bones – enough to impart the distinct taste of chalk!

RAGGED SCHOOL
1877

Anyone who knows London will have noticed those distinctive tall, red-brick, gothic-style schools – known originally as board schools. They were mostly built between 1880 and 1910 in a very similar and rather grand style as the very first attempt at mass education for the poor. At first, it is true, some of them charged sixpence a week, but soon even that charge was dropped and at last millions of poor Londoners began to be educated.

Before the establishment of these schools by the government, only the middle and upper classes who could pay – and it was expensive – were able to send their children to school, and then often only until the age of 12. Secondary education was solely for the elite, so London was home to millions of illiterate or semi-literate people who had no idea how to make the best of what little they had.

Even before this, however, there was a valiant attempt by a number of private charities to provide education for the poor. The ragged schools – or 'free schools' as they were known at the time – were the brainchild of Dubliner Thomas Barnardo. He had come to London intending to train as a doctor and missionary but was so appalled by the state in which the poor lived in London that he decided to do something about it. He opened a number of free schools including the Copperfield Road Free School in 1877.

For 30 years the school provided thousands of poor East End children with a free education. It closed in 1908 for the simple reason that the government had finally taken Barnardo's hint and set up enough government board schools to make Copperfield Road redundant. The school had been based in a series of old warehouses by the side of the Regent's Canal and after the school closed the warehouses were abandoned. Faced with demolition in the 1980s, they were saved by a group of local people who wanted to open a museum to remind the world how free education in London had really begun. As luck would have it, the buildings had never been modernised: instead, they have been kitted out with desks and blackboards once again and as a result they look just as they would have done a century and a half ago.

NEWGATE CELLS

1880

The Viaduct Tavern at Holborn is a glorious piece of Victorian architecture, one of the gin palaces that were so popular in London in the latter part of the nineteenth century, but according to some historians it has a dark secret. If you ask nicely, you may be shown the cellars, which, it is claimed, are actually part of the cells of the old Newgate Prison.

Certainly the pub is roughly in the right place and the cellars do have a prison-like feel to them, so the story may well be true – especially as at one time builders did tend to use cellars and foundations already in place when they constructed new buildings because it was cheaper than digging out new foundations and had no effect on the appearance of the exterior of the new building.

The only other place you can see a surviving part of the old Newgate Prison is at the end of Amen Corner near St Paul's, where a stretch of high wall remains.

GLADSTONE BAD

1882

In London's East End, close to Bow Church, there is a statue of William Ewart Gladstone (1809–98), the great nineteenth-century British prime minister. The statue is beautifully made, and the great orator stands, his hand outstretched, upon a fine marble plinth.

Few visitors to London, however, realise that this statue was paid for by the poor – and without their consent. What's more, they deeply resented having to pay for it. A short distance from the statue was a match factory owned by the Quakers Francis May and William Bryant. Quakers have a reputation among early industrialists for treating their workers well, but unfortunately that was not the case with Bryant and May. Their factory employed girls as young as ten to work 14-hour days for a pittance. The rules at work were also rigged to ensure that it was very difficult for the girls to avoid occasional infringements for which they were immediately fined – a way for their employers to make sure their wages were regularly less than they were owed.

In 1882, May and Bryant decided to contribute to funds to build the statue of Gladstone which we see today. However, instead of paying the money themselves, they deducted money from the wages of each of the several hundred girls who worked in the match factory. They did this without asking them – an act that was widely viewed, by the girls at least, as theft, and which led indirectly to the famous match-girl strike, which shut the Bow factory until conditions and pay were improved. Ironically the old factory now forms part of Bow Quarter, a luxury development of apartments – a far cry from the conditions known by the poor little match girls.

Another statue in London paid for in this underhand way was the Duke of York's Column in The Mall. Prince Frederick, Duke of York (1763–1827), was the second son of King George III and served as commander-in-chief of the British Army after 1795. The military setbacks that occurred under his watch were summarised in the nursery rhyme that mocked him: 'The Grand Old Duke of York'. When he died money was deducted from thousands of ordinary soldiers' pay to fund a monument dedicated to a man for whom they had little respect.

THE LOST GRAVEYARD

1885

Visitors to London don't often go to the Fulham Road, except perhaps if they are on their way to see the remains of the wonderful old Bishop's Palace by the river. The rest of Fulham is peculiarly lacking in interesting or historic buildings, despite the fact that centuries ago there were several splendid houses here. There is, however, an exception – one very strange survivor in this otherwise unexceptional area.

If you walk along Queen's Elm Parade, near the Royal Marsden Hospital on the Fulham Road, you will pass some high Victorian walls that appear to enclose nothing – or at least nothing requiring an entrance. Even local residents give the walls and the land they enclose almost no thought. Behind them, a smallish plot of ground has been largely unused and only rarely entered since as long ago as 1885. The story begins in 1815, when the Society of Jews paid £400 for this small patch of land in which they could bury their dead. At the time it was surrounded entirely by farms and meadows, which were famous for skylarks.

By 1885, after around 700 burials, the site – known as the Brompton Jewish Cemetery – had reached capacity. Once it was full, the gates were closed except to the relatives of the dead, but over the following century, the relatives of the dead themselves died and the place became largely forgotten. It remains an enigma – unvisited, forgotten and entirely inaccessible.

POSTMAN'S PARK

1887

London is famous across the world for its parks. Indeed, it would be a brave, not to say foolhardy, politician who suggested we build on any of the dozens of parks, both small and large, that still exist in every corner of the capital. Among the parks, of course, we must include that peculiarity of London – the square.

The idea for the typical London square was first realised in the late seventeenth century and continued well into the nineteenth. Houses were built around squares that were given over to gardens, gravelled walks and fountains, and many of these garden squares survive – some would say the fact that they are not generally open to the public is a great disadvantage, but actually this exclusivity ensures that the squares remain havens for wildlife.

Perhaps the most unusual open space in London is known as Postman's Park. Situated in the heart of the old City of London, bordered by Aldersgate Street, King Edward Street, Little Britain and St Martin's Le Grand, the park was once, like so many open spaces in the city, a burial ground – it was previously the churchyard of St Botolph's Aldersgate. The park encompasses the old graveyards of several churches – but most notably St Leonard, Foster Lane and Christ Church Greyfriars – as well as land made available after the demolition of old houses in Little Britain in 1880.

The park gets its odd name from its popularity among postmen, thousands of whom were formerly employed at the General Post Office headquarters nearby. But the strangest monument of all was placed here by the great Victorian painter G.F. Watts, whose house – a remarkable curiosity in its own right – still exists in Kensington. Watts was considered an important figure in his day, but by the 1960s his work was dismissed by critics and the public alike. A curious story tells of how, in the 1970s, his magnificent painting entitled *Hope* – now worth millions – was found in a terraced house in south London where it had been used to block an old chimney.

For reasons that are now obscure, Watts decided he would pay to affix decorative tiles to a wall in Postman's Park commemorating ordinary Londoners who had done extraordinary things. He was not interested in the rich and the famous, the powerful and the wealthy. Quite the contrary, in fact, for the tiles in the park celebrate the selfless deeds of people otherwise now completely forgotten. One of those commemorated is Joseph William Onslow, a lighterman, who was drowned at Wapping in the Thames while trying to save a boy's life. Another is Henry James Bristow who, in tearing off his sister's burning clothes, saved her life, only to lose his own when the flames engulfed him instead.

Watts had a fairly eccentric personal life. He married the famous actress Ellen Terry when she was just 16 and he was nearly 50. The marriage lasted little more than a year before Terry ran off with a younger man. And it was in 1887, while married to Scottish artist Mary Fraser Tytler (whom Watts had divorced once already and then remarried), that he decided to create his monument to ordinary heroic deeds. When he died in 1904, he had attached 13 tiles to the wall, but his widow continued to add tiles celebrating the deeds of ordinary people for many years. The last tile added was number 54.

ODD MAN OUT

1888

London is famously two cities, Westminster and the old City of London proper. Westminster Abbey is effectively the cathedral church of all London except the City, and St Paul's is the cathedral church of the Square Mile. Until relatively recently, this dual existence created a whole host of local rules and regulations that sometimes conflicted with one another, and it is still true to some extent that the City of London is not answerable to the monarch (and by extension her government at Westminster) in the same way as the rest of the country.

Thus, a free man of the City of London still cannot be hanged using a traditional hempen rope; he must be hanged using a silk rope. A free man can still drive his sheep over London Bridge without having to pay a toll, but if he tries this on Lambeth or Vauxhall Bridge he is liable to be arrested and his sheep confiscated.

As well as these examples, dozens of other strange rules have also survived that apply both in the City and in Greater London. By an Act of 1888, for example, all cyclists must ring their bells continuously while pedalling; pavements must never be used by anyone carrying a plank; you can be arrested for wearing a red coat if anyone suspects you are trying to impersonate a Chelsea Pensioner; and steam engines and other large vehicles of all kinds must be preceded by a man carrying a red flag (in daylight) or a red lantern (at night).

The rules about red flags and red lanterns continued to apply to buses and lorries whenever London was experiencing a pea-souper (dense fog), and until the 1960s on a dark foggy morning it was still common to see a bus or lorry slowly making its way along behind a swinging red lantern. None of these rules has ever actually been removed from the statute book, so beware!

TEMPERANCE CUPS
1888

The Victorian middle and upper classes were obsessed with the idea that the working classes were somehow a race apart. Social divisions in the nineteenth century were extraordinarily rigid and only very rarely, usually by dint of talent – as in the case of Charles Dickens – would the lower classes enter the glittering world of money and status.

The Victorian era was also one in which Christianity became more militant. The cosy Georgian world of the Anglican Church, where the poor accepted their place and the role of the clergy was to drink port and go to each other's houses for luncheon, was long gone. The church was keen to hunt down sin, and they saw alcohol as the chief corrupter of men's lives. It never occurred to them that the only respite the poor had from their harsh lives was the pub and their hard-earned drink at the end of a long day. So in the late nineteenth century Victorian London was a curious mix of huge, glamorous, brightly lit public houses (so-called gin palaces), which were built to encourage drinking, and the clergy, who denounced the evils of drink from the pulpit wherever they could.

One eccentric move by the Metropolitan Drinking Fountain Association to try to stop people drinking alcohol was to install elaborate stone drinking fountains next to or opposite the gin palaces. How they could have been so naïve as to think that water was ever likely to be a substitute for alcohol is difficult now to understand, but think it they did.

Some of these curious drinking fountains remain, but very few still have the tin cups on chains that were once found there. One well-preserved example does still exist, however, built into the railing of St Sepulchre's Church near Holborn Viaduct and close to one of the best-kept examples of the gin palace – the Viaduct Tavern. The drinking fountain has not one, but two old tin cups hanging from chains. They are now redundant as, presumably for reasons of hygiene, the water was turned off long ago.

MEMBERS' LAMP

1890

At the corner of Bridge Street and Parliament Square there is a stone pillar not unlike all the other stone pillars that run along the boundary of the Houses of Parliament, except that it is taller, and the observant will notice that it is topped with a curious glass lamp.

This lamp has been there since the days of horse-drawn hansom cabs at the end of the nineteenth century, and enables MPs to save time when they need a cab. They ring the Constable (as the relevant Palace of Westminster official is known) and tell him they will be leaving the office in, say, ten minutes. The Constable presses a button and the glass lamp starts to flash, telling any cab driver passing by that if he stops at the gate he will have the privilege of carrying an MP or minister home.

NANNIES IN THE DELL

1892

There is a delightful but little-noticed corner of Hyde Park that, until the Second World War, had the highest social cachet of anywhere in the park. On any given day in spring or summer the casual observer would have seen smartly dressed women with very large prams heading towards this corner of the park from the mansions of Mayfair and Belgravia. These women were not the mothers of the infants in their prams; they were full-time professional nannies employed by aristocratic women to take care of their children while they socialised and tried to do as little as possible. To have some form of employment meant that one was not out of the top drawer; real aristocrats were proud of the fact that they did nothing at all, and one result of this of course was that nannies had to be employed, generation after generation, to look after any children.

But the nannies that gathered in this corner of Hyde Park were no ordinary nannies. Rather like an army, they wore severe starched uniforms, heavy wool coats (even in summer) and absurd badges on their caps. They all dressed identically because their uniforms were supplied by the same aristocratic agency – the Norland Agency founded in 1892. They all pushed huge, expensive Silver Cross prams – like miniature sprung carriages – and on each the family crest would be prominently displayed. Such was the absurd snobbery associated with all this that only middle-class girls were accepted for nanny training, part of which included elocution lessons. Among their regular daily duties was wheeling their charges to Hyde Park or Kensington Gardens.

Even here, however, there were special rules, because not just anywhere in the park would do. When they reached the park the nannies and their charges were allowed through a set of gates into what was and is still known as the Dell. Here a beautifully kept lawn swept down through mature trees and shrubs to a tiny stream – a remnant of the old Westbourne River that was dug out in the eighteenth century to form the Serpentine. At the Knightsbridge end of the Serpentine, a culvert allows water to overflow under a bridge and down a short waterfall into the stream that runs next to the Dell before disappearing underground until it reaches the Thames near Chelsea Bridge.

Only nannies from the most aristocratic families with the largest gleaming prams (and wearing the correct uniform) were allowed into the Dell. More humble nannies, even those of wealthy families, were not allowed to sit in that idyllic spot. Once in the Dell, the nannies – famously dragon-like, according to the writer Eric Newby – would allow their charges to sit on the grass if it was very fine and to mix exclusively with babies from their own set. The absurdity of all this was ended by the Second World War, which made idleness seem far less admirable; allowing the already privileged to have even more privileges was regarded as rather absurd.

Today the Dell can be seen from the path that runs nearby, but it is closed to the public, and the beautiful lawns and mature trees play host only to the songbirds and the ghosts of those long-dead aristocratic children.

GHOSTLY STICKS

1892

A nineteenth-century newspaper recorded a bizarre discovery in the oldest part of the City of London, close to where the first London Bridge was built by the Romans. This area had for centuries revealed ancient coins and bits of statue, old timbers and silver, lead and even gold jewellery.

Workmen were said to enjoy repairing buildings on the riverfront because there was always a real chance of discovering a gold trinket, and in those days such finds would not be presented to a museum. Workmen were never paid well, and the discovery of anything valuable would be kept quiet and the artefact quickly melted down or otherwise disposed of.

In 1892 newspapers reported a discovery beneath an old house that didn't involve anything valuable, but was remarkable anyway. Workmen digging in a basement in that ancient tangle of houses and narrow alleys that once covered an area of ground close to the church of St Mary Woolnoth, near Bank Station, broke through some massive old stones that covered the basement floor, and found a set of narrow stone steps. They were able to descend only a short distance before their way was blocked by accumulated rubbish, but as they cleared this they found a few Tudor coins, a medieval pilgrim's badge and even an ancient leather shoe.

The builders cleared the rubbish and saw that the steps went down much further than they had initially thought, so they brought in some lights and, in a state of some excitement and no little fear, according at least to the contemporary newspaper report, they made their way down into the 'undiscovered gloom'.

At the bottom of the steps their flickering tapers discovered a small room in which the ashlar stone had been beautifully cut to create a barrel-shaped roof. The walls showed similarly fine work, as did the stones that comprised the floor. On one side of the strange room there was a low stone bench, and in a corner there was a great heap of what the workmen described as 'faggots' – by which they meant bundles of firewood – neatly tied and stacked.

At first the workmen thought the room was merely an old cellar, but it seemed to have been built too far down for that to make sense and, in any case, it was too grand. The sense that this room could have been Roman in origin increased when the men decided to move the solid-looking piles of firewood. 'At the first touch,' explained the workman to the newspaper, 'the heavy timber crumbled to dust in our fingers.' Clearly the wood had been in the room for so many centuries that, despite retaining its shape and the image of solidity, it had actually rotted away.

A TOWER IN
KENSINGTON
1894

One of the oddest architectural survivors in London can be found in South Kensington. Here, the whole area south of the Albert Memorial was designed by Victorian planners as a huge centre for the arts and sciences. This is where you will find the Victoria & Albert Museum, the Science Museum and the Natural History Museum within a street or two of one another.

The Royal College of Art is also based here, and the Royal Geographical Society has its delightful red-brick headquarters opposite Kensington Gardens, at the top of the appropriately named Exhibition Road. And close by is the magnificent Royal Albert Hall, the Victorians' vast circular homage to music. The modern buildings of Imperial College seem incongruous when viewed against the magnificence of these Victorian edifices, yet there they are, wedged between the Albert Hall and the Science Museum. How on earth did they get here?

The answer is because there was once another building here – the Imperial Institute. Completed in 1894, the Imperial Institute was a huge, part gothic, part Renaissance-style building very much in the style of the V&A and the Natural History Museum nearby. Built to promote research that could benefit the British Empire, in reality this meant finding ways to develop science and industry in the countries that were ruled by Britain. In 1899 it was taken over by the government, who let half of the building to the University of London for use as administrative offices, but by 1936 they had moved out.

Perhaps because the Empire had begun to diminish, in the 1950s the decision was taken to demolish the Imperial Institute. The building, in all its magnificence, was condemned and gradually torn down; the Imperial Institute morphed into the Commonwealth Institute, based in the old gardens of nearby Holland House. On the former site of the old Imperial Institute the new buildings of Imperial College that we see today were built. Rather like a gigantic public lavatory, they now surround the one part of the old Imperial Institute that was preserved – the huge ornate tower. The Queen's Tower as it is now known (originally it was called the Collcutt Tower, after its designer Thomas Edward Collcutt) is a staggering 285ft (87m) tall and one of London's lesser-known architectural gems.

In 2012 it was confirmed that the interior of the Commonwealth Institute would be converted by John Pawson to house the Design Museum following a move from its site at Shad Thames near Tower Bridge in 2016. The building received an £80 million makeover and the new museum, with over 107,639sq. ft (10,000sq. m) of exhibition space, will enrich the culture of this area even further.

TURKISH DELIGHT
1895

Wealthy travellers enjoying the Grand Tour during the eighteenth and nineteenth centuries returned to England and brought with them a taste for Turkish baths. At the time these were found not just in Turkey, to where the classically educated English gentleman would not usually have travelled, but also in Greece, which was then under Ottoman rule.

By the mid-nineteenth century, Turkish baths were all the rage in London and magnificent examples were built in Jermyn Street, Northumberland Avenue and elsewhere. They were often built in a Moorish style – with elaborate tiled walls, glittering mosaics and tinkling fountains. In the heart of the City there were several Turkish baths, and for a long time it was assumed none had survived. Then, in the early 1970s, Nevill's Turkish Baths in New Broad Street were rediscovered. The building had ceased to function as a baths in the early 1950s, when they went out of fashion, and for many years it was used as a storeroom, its marvellous interior gradually fading under decades of dust and dirt.

There had been a baths of some description in New Broad Street as early as 1817. The Argyll Medical Baths were established here in 1847, but as the name implies the idea was to offer baths as a cure for various ailments, rather than as a purely pleasurable experience. The addition of Turkish baths in 1860 was an acknowledgement that baths could be taken simply for the pleasure of a good scrub. Jones and Co. took over the baths in the 1880s, only to sell them on to James and Henry Forder Nevill in 1889. By 1895, the baths we see today had been built, and they were the last word in Moorish decadence.

After entering a small space at street level, the bather descended a winding staircase lined with gleaming colourful tiles to a small room in the basement where he bought his ticket. He then entered a cooling room where he could lie on a divan in a small cubicle, listen to the sound of a fountain and enjoy the Alhambra style of the decorative scheme. Beyond the cooling room were three increasingly warm rooms, all magnificently decorated with coloured tiles. The staircase was made of oak and the panels of walnut – this was a place of conspicuous luxury. So successful was the enterprise that, in 1908, the Nevills sold shares in the company. By this time they had baths at Whitechapel, London Bridge, Commercial Road and the Wool Exchange. So if you want to see one of the City's great survivors and eat where once London's wealthy lounged in Eastern luxury you can. Even if you don't go in, you can enjoy the visual excitement of the little Moorish kiosk with its tiles and arches and dome – all above ground and free for all to see.

LISTED PRISON BRICKS

1897

One of the strangest and most remarkable structures ever to be erected in London was the Milbank Prison. It was Europe's largest prison and the huge area it covered included the site where Tate Britain now stands near Vauxhall Bridge. The idea for the prison originated from the philosopher Jeremy Bentham, who put forward proposals for what he called his 'Panopticon Prison' – its basic design premise was that one guard could observe ('-opticon') on all ('pan-') the inmates at the same time.

The idea was to have a guard seated at the centre of a spider's web of corridors and cells. In practical terms, however, he would not actually be able to see into every cell at the same time, but the prisoners would never be sure that their cell was not the one being observed. Other than saving money on prison wardens, it is hard to know why Bentham thought this was a particularly useful idea, but then Bentham was an eccentric who famously asked that after death his body be sent to a taxidermist and his preserved remains propped up in a glass case at University College London, which he had helped to found. He thought the sense that they were always being watched would 'grind rogues into honest fellows'. Bentham's ideas were abandoned before the prison was built but they influenced the bizarre edifice that was built a decade later.

The new architect was clearly aware of Bentham's proposal because some aspects of the spider's web idea were incorporated. The eccentricities of the whole idea of a Milbank prison continued, however, when it was discovered that the man given the task of designing it was a former art master with no experience of building at all. His drawings were so bizarre it took three genuine architects to make sense of them and, over the following decade, get the job finished.

It had a central block with six sides, and going off in each direction were separate blocks that could only be reached through the main hub in the centre. The result was a building that looked like a giant snowflake. Despite the enormous amounts of time and money spent on it, Milbank Prison began to sink into the river mud almost from the day it was completed. The foundations were inadequate for such a huge building and one, moreover, that had been built on permanently soggy ground.

The proximity of the filthy river also meant prisoners died from frequent outbreaks of disease, so much so that eventually a new prison was built on higher ground at Pentonville in north London and Milbank was kept only for those prisoners awaiting transportation to Australia – a role Milbank continued to have until demolition began in 1892. Everyone whose ancestors were transported from England to Australia in the mid-nineteenth century would have walked down the river steps from the prison, stepped on to a boat to be taken across the ocean, probably for the rest of their lives.

But one extraordinary thing rose from the ruins of the prison. For centuries this had been a very poor part of London – it was an extension, if you like, of the Devil's Acre slum area in nearby Westminster – so a decision was made to reuse the millions of bricks from the prison to build more than 4,000 working people's flats. These flats comprise the Milbank Estate, which has hardly been altered since first being built between 1897 and 1902. Indeed, so well made are the flats that they are now listed by English Heritage as being of special historic interest. Also, as a nice touch, the flats were named after famous English painters, including Turner and Hogarth.

Nearby, and also listed, is the old Army Medical College building, where the world's first effective typhoid vaccine was discovered. Set around a square where the soldiers once paraded, the college buildings are now used by an art college, but they have not been altered.

A few other traces of the old prison remain. On the edge of the Milbank flats nearest Vauxhall Bridge Road there is what looks like a deep ditch running for about 100 yards – this is the last section of the perimeter ditch from the original prison. And on the riverside nearby is another survivor: a heavy stone bollard which once stood at the top of the river steps down which so many prisoners descended at the start of their journey to Australia. It is said they would brush their hand across the top of the bollard as they passed: a last touch of England.

GRUESOME RELICS

1901

The outskirts of London were once dotted with convents and monasteries. Many sprang up during the nineteenth century after theologian John Henry Newman converted to Catholicism and made it respectable and even fashionable. This was a remarkable sea change for, in the eighteenth century, following the Glorious Revolution of 1688–89 and the establishment of a line of Protestant monarchs, Catholics were still occasionally persecuted and they were banned from many professions.

Of course, this didn't stop aristocratic families such as the Dukes of Norfolk retaining the old religion, but for ordinary Catholics life could be difficult. But a gradual liberalisation of society, combined with a passion for gothic art and architecture, slowly made Catholicism seem more solidly English than Anglicanism, which had, after all, been established to a large extent by Henry VIII, a most unattractive man whose main hobby appears to have been disposing of his wives.

Once Catholicism was back in fashion, Westminster Cathedral was built on Francis Street near London Victoria Station, along with hundreds of other new Catholic churches up and down the country. Close to Marble Arch, in Hyde Park Place, a small Catholic convent was established in 1901, and remarkably, despite the closure of so many of these suburban convents, this one still survives.

What makes the Tyburn Convent especially interesting is that the nuns set up their convent here to be near the site where so many Catholics had been killed for their faith. The nuns live a largely silent life, for this is a strict order, officially known as The Benedictine Adorers of the Sacred Heart of Jesus of Montmartre, founded in 1898. The convent has 12 sister houses around the world and the order follows the rule of St Benedict. Nuns wear traditional habits and though it is not strictly a silent order, there are long periods of silence every day.

This curious medieval survival in west London is made stranger still by the relics the convent contains. Above the altar in the chapel, too, is a gruesome reminder of the past: a reproduction of the Tyburn gallows, where more than 100 Catholic martyrs were killed. The Catholic passion for relics can be seen here in all its glory: the convent's collection includes a small piece of linen and some straw stained with the blood of five Catholics killed at Tyburn in the seventeenth century; there is a finger from John Roberts who was hanged, drawn and quartered at Tyburn in 1610; a lock of hair from an unidentified martyr; and, perhaps most gruesome of all, a fingernail from the Jesuit Thomas Holland, who died at Tyburn in December 1642.

FINAL STEPS

1902

The area towards the western end of Fleet Street, where the Old Bailey (otherwise known as the Central Criminal Court) now stands, has a dark and ancient history. The Victorian court buildings were built on part of the site of the old Newgate Prison, at one time one of the most notorious prisons in Europe. Hangings were a regular public occurrence until 1868, and many of those who were hanged were buried under the floor of Dead Man's Walk, a path between the jail and the old court. The riots that took place on hanging days were such that a secret tunnel was built between the court and nearby St Sepulchre's Church so that the priest could speak to the condemned before his or her execution without being abused by the crowd.

Rebuilt and remodelled numerous times, but especially after the Great Fire of 1666, the current buildings date from 1902, but even this relatively modern building retains a gruesome eccentricity. The corridor from the condemned cells to the room where executions took place until very recently was built in a most unusual way: as you walk out of the cell the ceiling is of a normal height and the walls leave a wide pathway ahead. Within 20 paces, however, the ceiling height becomes steadily lower until it is necessary to stoop; the walls close in gradually on each side until there is barely space for someone to pass by. The idea was to remind the condemned that death was closing in on them.

HIGH DAYS
AT THE HOTEL
1902

The early 1960s saw the destruction of one of the capital's most marvellous landmarks, but it was a landmark with a difference and one little known outside a relatively small circle. The Cavendish Hotel in Mayfair had been based in three adjoining Regency houses in Jermyn Street (and the corner of Duke Street) since at least the mid-nineteenth century. Then, in 1902, a young woman who had already made a name for herself as a cook heard that the lease of the hotel was about to run out and that the proprietor wanted to retire. The young woman decided this was her chance.

Rosa Lewis was born in London's East End in 1867. She went to a local board school, schools established to provide places for London's poor, and began work as a kitchen maid at the age of 12. She was very good-looking, very quick-witted and learned fast. Soon she was working as a cook in her own right. She worked for Mrs Randolph Churchill and then moved to France, where she became famous for her menus. Back in England a few years later, she found herself much in demand. Edward VII, with whom she was rumoured to have had an affair, insisted she cook for him, and she travelled all over the country with him together with a team she hand-picked. While working for Winston Churchill's mother, she was pestered in the kitchen by the young Winston until, goaded beyond endurance, she shouted, 'Hop it, Copper Knob' at him.

For Rosa Lewis that was mild language, for she was famously and hilariously foul-mouthed. Even in the days of her wealth and fame she continued to go to Covent Garden market each morning at 5a.m. to buy the freshest fruit and vegetables. But her fame as an extraordinary character as well as a talented cook really began to spread when she took over the Cavendish Hotel. Within a year, the establishment was attracting a rich and aristocratic clientele, despite the fact that it was shabby and filled with eccentric items of furniture. One guest recalled that it was like a magnificent but rather dirty and run-down country house. Huge sofas were combined with old rugs and painted floorboards, rickety old pieces of furniture leaned against crooked walls and dogs seemed to be asleep everywhere. Rosa divided part of the hotel into suites where the very rich and well-connected, including the king, could entertain in private.

The aristocrats who stayed at the Cavendish became Rosa's friends, and she would accompany them to the opera – an extraordinary thing in early twentieth-century London, when servants were usually treated as if they simply did not exist. Her admirers, including Lord Ribblesdale, who was devoted to her, regularly sent her cartloads of flowers, which she promptly sent on to any of her friends who happened to be in hospital or prison. Anyone down on their luck would be allowed to stay free of charge – sometimes for years – and she would charge their bills to her super-rich clients, who barely seemed to notice. If they did complain she would say 'Don't worry about that; it will all come out in the wash.'

She herself drank nothing but champagne and was utterly fearless in defence of those she liked, but she would terrify those she didn't take to with a string of the foulest expletives. As she grew older, she grew more eccentric and would deliberately mispronounce her guests' names or pretend she had mistaken them for someone else.

Rosa became so wealthy she was able to buy a country house but, having thrown her drunken husband out of the hotel soon after it opened, she never remarried, preferring instead the company of her lifelong friend Edith. Much of the hotel was decorated with old empty jeroboams of champagne, their labels signed by the great and the good. Rosa also loved going to salerooms and would buy ridiculously impractical items – a stuffed rhinoceros, a set of huge Gobelin tapestries (which turned out to be fakes) and, maddest of all, a huge set of gates from Dorchester House in Park Lane when it was demolished in the 1920s.

Rosa Lewis's Cavendish was said to be the most entertaining place in London. It even housed a full-blown aristocratic prostitute, who stayed free of charge provided she continued to provide gentlemen's services. If any of Rosa's guests decided not to use her services and instead picked a girl up in Piccadilly, Rosa would shout at them when they returned to the hotel: 'We'll get the doctor to look at your winkle in the morning.'

'She always did it when there were others milling about in the hall,' recalled one of her regulars, 'to maximise the embarrassment and teach you never to do it again!'

When Rosa died in her sleep in 1952, aged 85, the hotel carried on for another decade, but changing tastes and changing times led to a decline in the hotel's popularity and it was forced to close in 1962. The new owners promised they would at least retain the buildings (or their façades – the hotel was comprised of several beautiful old houses that had been knocked together), but they went back on their word and the old hotel was razed to the ground, to be replaced by the infinitely dull Cavendish Hotel that stands on the site today.

CHRIST'S HOSPITAL RATS

1905

Christ's Hospital School (one of a number of charitable Bluecoat Schools – named after the colour of the boys' uniforms) was attached to a large gothic hall situated between King Edward Street and Giltspur Street.

Built in 1825 and modelled on the chapel of King's College Cambridge, the hall was demolished – despite widespread protest – in 1905. It was generally agreed to be one of the city authorities' worst acts of vandalism.

The school had already moved to Horsham in Sussex, where it remains, but when the school left a great and very odd tradition died. This was that all schoolboys should catch one or more of the rats for which the hall was famous. This was all very well but it was considered unmanly to catch them with terriers or in traps – the poor boys had to catch them with their bare hands!

HACKED OFF
1908

Compared to the French, the British have always been very prudish. The Victorians famously covered the legs of their tables, and no one in polite society would ever even use the words 'legs' if it could possibly be avoided.

A citizen of Lewes in Sussex, an art collector called E.P. Warren, commissioned a version of Rodin's marvellous sculpture *The Kiss* at the beginning of the twentieth century. The work – now famous the world over – is known by the same name as Rodin's, but it was rejected as too pornographic at the time. The campaign against it was led by the wonderfully named Miss Fowler-Tutt, and no doubt Lewes would love to have it back now!

One of the city's oddest tales concerning sculptures that offended the public taste concerns the figures on what is now Zimbabwe House on the Strand. Jacob Epstein (1880–1959) was an avant-garde artist who had already been commissioned to produce a statue for Lewis's department store in Liverpool. The resulting figure was so well endowed that it was quickly dubbed 'Dickie Lewis', but this doesn't seem to have worried the architect who commissioned Epstein's work for Zimbabwe House (then the British Medical Association Headquarters). For Epstein it was a huge commission – 18 large nude figures were to be distributed across the façade of the new building.

The architect seems to have gone ahead with the project without a qualm, even when the striking nudity of the carvings became apparent, but when the building was finally unveiled in 1908 there was uproar. Letters were written to *The Times* complaining that young women would be corrupted by the disgusting display of nakedness. One correspondent insisted that he would sue the architect and the BMA under the Obscenity Act. The complaints gradually died down and the statues were left *in situ*, but then in the 1930s the more prominent parts of the statues were quietly hacked off on the grounds that the statues (or their bigger bits) had become unstable and there was a danger that 'anything sticking out' might fall on the heads of passers-by!

Further commissions for the London Electric Tramway building in 1929 caused Epstein even more problems. This bizarre-looking lump of a building near St James's Park included two nude statues, known as *Night* and *Day*, and as usual there were complaints about them being too sexual. Modifications were made, the easily offended went away at last, but public commissions for Epstein finally dried up.

DOCTOR WHO
AT EARL'S COURT

1910

Fans of the television series *Doctor Who* often come to London and are hugely disappointed that there are no longer any blue police telephone boxes to be found – the boxes that were the model for the original TARDIS.

From around 1910 until the 1960s there were hundreds of these curious-looking phone boxes all over London. But a vast increase in the number of ordinary telephone boxes made the old blue boxes largely redundant and gradually they were dismantled and disposed of.

The arrival of walkie-talkies and then mobile phones sealed the fate of the last few of these wonderfully evocative call boxes. But, against all the odds, one such box does remain, and it can be found just outside Earl's Court Station in west London.

TAKING LIBERTIES

1910

Until 1917, one of London's most picturesque streets was Cloth Fair in the delightfully named ward of Farringdon Within (meaning within the old City walls). This narrow street runs from Little Britain to Middle Street, a distance of just 150 yards (137m), and along the side of the old Church of St Bartholomew the Great, one of London's least altered and most ancient churches. In 1917, almost all the old houses in Cloth Fair were pulled down. Just one seventeenth-century house survives today, but it has been so over-restored that you might easily think it modern.

But Cloth Fair still has a curious tale to tell for, tiny though it is, it was, until around 1910, a liberty. In medieval times a liberty was an area of land that was under the control of the king, and that control was devolved either to a bishop or local nobleman. For centuries thereafter an area designated a liberty had its own rules and system of governance, and was exempt from any restrictions or rules implemented via local government in the area surrounding it. This led to some very odd situations. In south London at Southwark, for example, the Clink Prison and much of the area surrounding it was run as a sort of personal fiefdom by the Bishop of Winchester, who used his powers to run and profit from a series of brothels.

Cloth Fair was even more remarkable in that it survived the Local Government Act of 1888 which abolished many of the remaining liberties up and down the country. Then, in 1910, Cloth Fair, which until that date closed its gates against the world each night, decided it needed street lighting and to be connected to the sewage system. It did not have enough money to do this on its own. The only way to modernise was to join the surrounding local council. The Liberty of Cloth Fair then ceased to exist, but the delightful narrow road can still be found, with its ancient church and the former home of poet John Betjeman.

FREE BOOKS

1911

One of England's most bizarre pieces of legislation is the 1911 Copyright Act, which decrees that a number of British libraries are entitled to receive a copy of every book, magazine and newspaper published in England free of charge. Although enshrined in the 1911 Act, the right to these copies actually dates back – astonishingly – to 1662.

The idea originally had more to do with censorship than preserving the knowledge and experience of the nation for future generations, which is usually given as the justification for the practice today.

It began when the Stationers' Company – a London guild that had regulated book and other publications since the 1400s – agreed with Sir Thomas Bodley that new books should always be sent to the Bodleian Library in Oxford. At the time, this was the pre-eminent British library – the British Library as we know it now did not yet exist.

The requirement to send books to the Bodleian was enshrined in law in the Statute of Anne, 1710. Today the five legal deposit libraries are the Bodleian in Oxford, Cambridge University Library, the National Library of Scotland, the library of Trinity College, Dublin, and the National Library of Wales. But by a quirk in the legislation, only the British Library now receives a copy of every publication by right. The others must be sent new books and magazines, but only if they request them. The irony of the system is that it was designed to meet the needs of an age when relatively few books were published – in the eighteenth century probably only a few thousand books a year at most were published in England.

By the late nineteenth century, mass book production meant the copyright libraries (and of course especially the British Library) were receiving tens of thousands of new books each year. By the 1990s, that figure had reached hundreds of thousands a year, as the libraries felt obliged to keep copies not just of new books, but of new editions of books already published.

The British library has over 388 miles (625km) of shelves, and grows by 7½ miles (12km) every year. It can take two days for a book ordered by a reader to arrive at his or her desk! A decision was taken recently to try to store more books digitally, but there is resistance to this as in many ways a book, though fragile, is not as fragile as data on a disk.

TWEAKING
NAPOLEON'S NOSE
1912

The large semicircular building at the Trafalgar Square entrance to the Mall has a curious history. It was commissioned by King Edward VII in memory of his mother Queen Victoria, and completed in 1912. The architect was Sir Aston Webb, who also re-fronted Buckingham Palace just down the road.

Successive governments have been allowed the use of a flat in Admiralty Arch, but it is now mostly used as offices. It also has another curious feature.

There are four arches through the building: two for pedestrians and two central arches for road traffic. On the wall of the northern traffic arch, some 6ft (1.8m) off the ground, a life-size brass nose sticks out of the stonework. The nose is at just the right height to be clearly visible to anyone passing who happens to be riding a horse and, given that horse transport still dominated London when the building was completed, when it was first spotted people did think that it could have been one of Edward VII's little jokes.

He was certainly fond of gags and the theory was that Edward had the nose designed in the shape of Napoleon's so that passing cavalry officers (and anyone else on horseback) could give it a good tweak or a punch as they passed by.

However, it is actually one of a number of plaster of Paris noses that were placed in different locations around London by artist Rick Buckley in 1997.

MILKING IT

1913

Milk only began to reach London in large quantities in the 1850s and 1860s, when the railway network had become sufficiently widespread and reliable to supply the vast quantities of milk consumed in the capital each day. However, old habits die hard, as the saying goes, and many people preferred to get their milk locally long after it was either necessary or hygienic.

Until well into the twentieth century, large numbers of cattle were still kept in central London, and often in the most astonishing conditions. The Adelphi, built by the three Adam brothers between 1768 and 1772, was just east of Charing Cross Station: a magnificent Neo-classical building (actually a terrace of 24 houses grouped together) that stretched along the river frontage. For a time after it was built, the Adelphi was immensely fashionable and only the wealthy could afford to live there.

But, as the area around Charing Cross declined, the rich began to move out. By the mid-nineteenth century, the grand rooms at the Adelphi were being let to anyone who could be enticed by low rents to live there. But even its most unfashionable residents might have been astonished at what went on in its cellars, for it was here, deep underground, that a whole herd of cows was kept. They were permanently housed inside the basement of the building and fed entirely on waste from the brewing industry. As a result, they produced a lot of milk, but their feed turned the milk blue and it had to be mixed with normal milk to make it sellable.

Many other London houses were used to keep cows. The owner of a terraced house in Islington was fined in 1890 for keeping too many cows in his house. Note that the problem was not the presence of cows, but simply that there were too many! The smell and the noise of one or two cows would have been fine, but half a dozen began to annoy the neighbours. The owner of the house kept the cows on the first floor and slept with his family on the second floor. A visitor described seeing three cows happily munching hay in a sitting room with a fine big marble fireplace just behind them!

A TYPEFACE IN THE RIVER

1913

A few hundred yards upstream from Hammersmith Bridge, along a footpath that looks pretty much today as it did a century and more ago and down a narrow alleyway, there is a tiny public house. This is The Dove, an eighteenth-century house whose snug bar, measuring around 8 × 8ft (2.4 × 2.4m), is one of the smallest in the country. The pub was also the inspiration for one of London's oddest disputes.

At the beginning of the twentieth century, the bookbinder T.J. Cobden-Sanderson and his partner Emery Walker set up the Doves Press, just along the river from and named after The Dove public house. Cobden-Sanderson was a friend of William Morris and active supporter of the Arts and Crafts movement. The press, which inspired many other similar private independent presses, was an attempt to take bookmaking back from the big impersonal printers who had turned bookbinding from a craft into an industrial process.

For eight years, from 1900–08, the partners seem to have got on famously. Walker seems to have been the main designer of the famous Doves Press font; every one of the press's books was designed using this typeface and always in the same size. When the two men fell out, Walker managed to wrest an agreement from his former partner that the rights to the typeface would revert to Walker when Cobden-

Sanderson died. But the legal agreement neglected to mention ownership of the pieces of metal type themselves, and the matrices – the moulds from which the metal type was made. If they were lost or destroyed then the rights to the typeface would be meaningless. Clearly the spat was a particularly nasty one, because Cobden-Sanderson decided early in 1913 to make sure Walker would never get his hands on the physical type.

At midnight on 21 March that year, Cobden-Sanderson began throwing all the matrices into the River Thames from the middle of Hammersmith Bridge. A few years later he recorded in his journal that he disposed of the metal type in the river too – there was so much of it that it took 177 trips! History does not record Walker's reaction to this – presumably he found out in the end – but all was not lost. In 2015, Robert Green recreated the typeface and then searched the riverbed under Hammersmith Bridge to recover hundreds of pieces of the original type.

For a long time Hammersmith Terrace was the home of William Morris and other Arts and Crafts movement enthusiasts, but especially typographers. The Dove remains today as a reminder of those heady days more than a century ago, along with the Emery Walker Museum at 7 Hammersmith Terrace, one of London's most obscure museums and the last perfect Arts and Crafts interior in existence. This splendid eighteenth-century house contains the huge collection of furniture and objects amassed by Walker and preserved by his daughter Dorothy, who died in 1963. The house and its contents survived intact because Dorothy left it to her lifelong companion Elizabeth De Haas, who died as recently as 1999, leaving the house and its contents in trust.

HORSE AND MOTOR
1915

Barbon Close is named after one of London's greatest developers. Born around 1640, Nicholas Barbon was trained as a physician but became a brilliant financier and property developer who funded large areas of speculative building west of the City of London.

Perhaps the oddest thing about Barbon, however, was his middle name. His father had him christened Nicholas If-Jesus-Christ-Had-Not-Died-For-Thee-Thou-Hadst-Been-Damned Barebone!

Barbon Close can be found a short distance to the east of the British Museum and near the ancient lawyers' inns, and at the corner of Barbon Close is a very odd building: an eighteenth-century house still with its eighteenth-century shop window on the ground floor and a large hand-painted sign hanging on the wall nearby. This sign, which is still in remarkably good condition, states proudly that this is the premises of G. Bailey & Sons, Horse & Motor Contractors. The survival of the sign, a century and more after horses vanished from the streets of London, is testament to Londoners' love of the past.

MOVING HOUSE

1930

One of the saddest and strangest stories regarding London houses concerns Lansdowne House, which originally stood at the south-west corner of Berkeley Square. A beautiful house built by Robert Adam in the classical style and completed in 1763, the house had a large forecourt and its garden stretched across the whole of the bottom half of Berkeley Square. This meant that the Devonshires, who owned Devonshire House on Piccadilly, had an unimpeded view across the garden of Lansdowne House to the square itself.

In 1930, in an act of vandalism now impossible to understand, Westminster City Council decided that keeping a magnificent house was of far less importance than encouraging the use of the car, so a plan was hatched to demolish the whole of the front of the house, along with all the front rooms – all of which had been decorated magnificently by Adam. As a result, a road now runs where these priceless rooms were once laid out, and the house's former gardens were taken in order to build two huge office blocks. Meanwhile, a shabby version of the front of the house was rebuilt 30ft (9.1m) back from its original position, and the magnificent drawing room and dining room were shipped off to American museums.

Today, the sad remains of the house have been turned into the Lansdowne Club. When the club's owners took over from the Petty-Fitzmaurice family, who had owned the house from 1761 until the early 1930s, the club redesigned much of the interior in an Art Deco style, but one or two Adam rooms still remain. Famous residents or owners of the house include at least three prime ministers (including William Pitt the Younger), the artist Beryl Cook and Gordon Selfridge of department store fame.

WATERLOO WOMEN

1939

It is a sad truism that if there is a beautiful building or structure in London, there will be someone who would like to redevelop it – a word often used to make destruction sound like something positive. But one would have thought that a bridge across the Thames that had been celebrated in paintings by Constable and Monet, not to mention being the subject of a fine poem by Thomas Hood, might have escaped. Unfortunately not.

John Rennie's magnificent Georgian Waterloo Bridge, completed in 1817, had nine arches, each separated by pairs of splendid Doric pillars. It was highly decorative and widely admired. London County Council, notoriously blind to the virtues of London architecture, gave the go-ahead to demolish it in the 1930s. The rather plain, functional bridge that replaced it still stands, but it is a little-known fact that it was largely built by women.

The female crew was drafted in between 1939 and 1945, when the new bridge was finally completed. By the standards of the time, women doing the sort of heavy manual work involved in bridge-building was remarkable, but by then the war was on and almost every able-bodied man in the country had been called up. Yet there was still a great deal of embarrassment about the whole thing, if the opening ceremony is anything to go by. The women's contribution was not acknowledged in any of the speeches on the day, and none of the women who had worked on the bridge were invited to attend. Labour minister Herbert Morrison said: 'The men who built Waterloo Bridge are fortunate men. They know that, although their names may be forgotten, their work will be a pride and use to London for many generations to come.' It was all very peculiar, and the mystery deepened when building contractor Peter Lind and Co., who had worked with architect Giles Gilbert Scott on the bridge, went out of business and all their records were destroyed in the early 1980s.

LIFE IN THE CHURCH TOWER

1940

War-damaged churches were often rebuilt, and in some cases great efforts were made to replicate the internal features that had been destroyed. St James's Church in Piccadilly is a good example. Other churches were left in their damaged state, or their towers were retained while the rest of the church was demolished.

Christ Church Greyfriars, which was also sometimes known as Christ Church Newgate Street, is a case in point. The name Greyfriars refers to the habits worn by the Franciscan monks who lived in the attached monastery, but worshipped at the church. The priory buildings were also home to Christ's School, a foundation that survives but moved out of London long ago.

By the early 1930s, the congregation at Christ Church Greyfriars had declined to a few dozen, and then, on 29 December 1940, a firebomb destroyed the church including all its fittings – with one extraordinary exception. For reasons even he could not later explain, a passing fireman ran into the burning church and rescued the beautifully carved, late seventeenth-century wooden font cover. He said afterwards that he felt a strange compulsion to run into the church, despite the danger, and though he had never previously been inside and knew nothing of the contents, he felt the font cover had to be saved.

Perhaps the strangest thing about this church, however, is that the tower, which survived the fire, was taken apart stone by stone after the war ended and then reassembled in exactly the same place. The idea was to strengthen it with modern building materials including steel beams. Inevitably, as this was the 1960s, part of the old churchyard – which had been the site of the medieval monastery – was taken for street widening and then in 1981 an office block (equally inevitably) was built in the south-west corner of the old churchyard. The rebuilt tower was converted into several flats, which are inhabited to this day. So, if you want to live in a Wren-designed tower in central London, keep an eye on local estate agents...

GOING NOWHERE

1942

During the Blitz, London was heavily bombed in a series of night-time raids that went on for weeks at a time, and left large parts of the capital in ruins. The worst part of the bombing was that it was aimed not just at military targets – the railways and the docks, for example – but also at civilian areas.

The bombing became part of everyday life, and rather than weakening the resolve of Londoners to stay in their city, it strengthened it. But the night-time raids meant huge disruption, with thousands of families spending night after night underground in the Tube stations, in factory and office basements and even, occasionally, in parts of the sewer system.

The bombs uncovered some very unusual, long-forgotten features of the capital, including stretches of Roman wall that had been hidden in the basements of old houses, but one or two other architectural oddities were revealed that have never been explained. A street of late-Victorian houses in south London was thought to be pretty much like any other urban street until one night in 1942 a group of bombers heading back to Germany released their unused bombs just to get rid of them and lighten their aircraft. The bombs fell on a tall, red-brick Victorian house, scoring a direct hit and blowing out the whole of the façade, which left the house looking rather like one of those dolls' houses that allow you to remove the front to see what is inside.

When the rescue services and firemen arrived in the street as dawn broke, they were surprised but also relieved to discover that no one appeared to have been in the house when it was hit. When they began to search more carefully, they realised this was a very peculiar house indeed. Incredibly, most of the furniture was still standing in the various rooms – the force of the blast appeared to have been taken entirely by the front wall. All the furniture appeared to be ancient – mid-Victorian in the main. There was nothing odd about that in itself – many people kept their inherited furniture and only rarely bought new things at a time when money was tight and the idea of constantly modernising was still decades in the future. But even by the standards of the time, the furniture and pictures in the house seemed ancient.

Shocked neighbours were able to confirm that no one had been seen entering or leaving the house for years, and the curtains were always shut. It was simply assumed that the owners lived elsewhere and couldn't let the house or perhaps just didn't want to. No one had thought anything of it. In the basement of the house, an old black range was still *in situ*, despite the fact that gas cookers were almost universal by this time. Thick dust lay everywhere in the kitchen, and it was not the sort of brick and plaster dust one might have expected after an explosion. It was the sort of dust that gathers slowly over many years, and only when a room is left entirely undisturbed.

At the back of the kitchen came the strangest thing of all. An old, thick-planked door led into a brick-vaulted tunnel that led under the garden at the back of the bombed house, across another garden and then on into the basement of another very similar house in the next street. The tunnel had been blocked just at the point where it should have entered the basement of the other house, and the owners of the house to which it led were entirely unaware that a tunnel had been dug between their house and the bombed house nearby.

With war raging and the threat of air raids ever present, few enquiries were made about this odd house, but eventually someone came forward and claimed to be related to the owners. He insisted the details of the house and its owners were all held by a firm of solicitors in the city, but when this information was followed up it was discovered that the solicitor's office had also been bombed and all the deeds and other paperwork held by the firm had been destroyed. The mystery of the suburban house and the tunnel was never solved.

WARTIME HIDEOUTS

1942

During the Second World War, so many German bombs were dropped on London that a map recently created to show where they fell left little or no spaces at all between the bomb sites (see www.bombsight.org), so in a sense it is remarkable that so much did survive. Thousands of Londoners died during the Blitz, and this period of destruction led to thousands more being made homeless.

But, far fewer people died than had been expected. One of the reasons for the relatively low numbers of casualties was that the London Underground system was used as a night-time shelter. And not just the Underground – the Turkish baths under London's exclusive Dorchester Hotel were also used, as was the huge underground banqueting hall at the Savoy. Here, according to legend, a special area was created for 'persistent and serious snorers'! But the Underground hid more than just civilians.

Until the 1980s, it was still a carefully guarded government secret that almost 5 miles (8km) of the Central Line was being used during the war to manufacture thousands of tons of armaments. Much of the know-how and equipment was provided and maintained by the arms company Plessey.

So sophisticated was the operation that entire fighter planes were also made in the tunnels. The Piccadilly Line was used to store thousands of art treasures and historic artefacts from the British Museum and various London churches.

CHURCHILL IN A BUCKET

1942

Winston Churchill was famous for many things, not least his remarkable ability to inspire the British people to believe that however badly things were going in the war they should not give up hope. He certainly had a presence, a bulldog quality remarked on by all his biographers, and he would go to great lengths to show the population of London in particular that whatever the Germans threw at them, they would get up, dust themselves down and carry on.

This spirit of determination led to one comic incident that did nothing to lessen Churchill's reputation. In 1942, while on a tour of one of London's worst-hit areas during the Blitz, Churchill was surrounded by a huge mob of admirers. He had been talking to a group of firemen and rescue workers, who explained to him that the bombs had not only flattened the surrounding houses, but had also damaged the massive Victorian sewers beneath their feet.

Churchill was fascinated by this and immediately asked if he could examine the damaged sewers himself. The only way to do this, explained the firemen, was to be lowered by crane in a large metal bucket. The firemen were convinced Churchill would leave it at that but, ever the eccentric, he immediately demanded that a portable crane be brought over to the huge hole in the ground. He was helped into the bucket, which was suspended from a thick chain and, smiling broadly and making his characteristic victory salute, was lowered into the sewer. His assistants later explained that he was rather embarrassed on reaching the bottom of the hole to discover that there was absolutely nothing to see, but, rather than be hauled up to the waiting crowd immediately, he sat in the bucket for ten minutes, smoking his cigar, before shouting to be hauled back up. The crowd, as can be expected, was most impressed.

CATFORD PREFABS
1945

After the Second World War there was a feeling in Britain that the country should not be allowed to return to the old pre-War world where the poor simply had to put up with damp, unheated houses and low wages. This stemmed from the fact that the working classes had provided most of the soldiers who fought the Nazis, and that they deserved better, especially as so many among the upper classes had quietly sent their sons to Ireland and elsewhere to avoid them having to be called up.

But, of course, there was a major problem – so many houses had been destroyed by German bombers, especially in London, that it wasn't a question of better housing so much as a question of any housing at all. Such was the shortage that the government came up with the idea of building prefabs – prefabricated houses that would be quick and cheap to put up. Assembled in a few days from factory-made panels, prefabs sprang up all over the country, and with their small gardens and neat, cosy appearance, they were a huge success. But, as they were meant to last only a decade or so, almost all have now been demolished. But in Catford, in south-east London, the last big estate of prefabs survived, incredibly, until 2014.

What makes the Excalibur Estate unusual and interesting is that the panels, chimneys, floors, ceilings and other components of these houses were delivered by lorries driven by German and Italian prisoners of war, who then helped put the pieces together. Though the Excalibur Estate has been demolished, six prefabs were saved by English Heritage to create a museum where you could see a typical prefab, its interior decorated just as it would have been in the 1940s and 1950s.

Sadly, seven months after the museum opened in 2014, an arson attack forced its closure. Since then the team behind the museum were able to secure Heritage Lottery funding to support Moving Prefab, which allowed them to take their knowledge, photographs, recordings and documents on the road, and share the history and experiences of the Excalibur Estate and its residents with enthusiasts around the country.

BLACK BRICKS IN OLD QUEEN STREET

c.1950

No. 26 Old Queen Street in Westminster is a beautiful Georgian house which – rarely these days – has kept at least some of its Georgian interiors. It lies on a road that runs into an even older street – Queen Anne's Gate – arguably the most beautiful street in London. But No. 26 is interesting and rather special for the oddest of reasons.

Its strangeness dates back to a time before the Clean Air Acts of the 1950s and 1960s, which banned the use of coal for domestic heating. The idea was to rid London of its wonderfully atmospheric but dangerous and unhealthy fogs known as 'pea-soupers'. These fogs, made famous by Whistler and other artists who saw romance and mystery in the murky gloom, caused thousands of deaths among the elderly and infirm each year.

The fog also ensured that almost every house in London quickly turned black after being built – so much so that it became fashionable to have a house with black bricks, ideally just the right shade of 'soot black'. After the Second World War, when the Prime Minister's house at No. 10 Downing Street was altered, it was decided to clean the external bricks. The result looked so awful that the bricks were immediately painted black to recreate the dirty look they'd had before. And, to this day, the bricks of No. 10 are always painted black.

No. 26 Old Queen Street is rather similar, but its bricks are kept black by being washed in a special solution that is filled with genuine coal dust. The work is carried out by English Heritage, which tries, against overwhelming odds, to protect the few interesting old buildings left in London. No. 26 is interesting for another reason, too, for this was once the house where the monarch's falconer lived. This was a highly prestigious job because until the end of the eighteenth century falconry really was the sport of kings. The king's falconer was so important that he was the only person, besides the royal family itself, allowed to drive along Birdcage Walk, which runs just behind Old Queen Street.

A BIRD AT THE CORONATION

1953

Osborne de Vere Beauclerk, 12th Duke of St Albans, inherited his title as a direct result of the fact that his ancestor, Nell Gwyn, gave birth to the illegitimate son of Charles II. Legend has it that the dukedom was created for the 14-year-old Charles Beauclerk after his mother, in the king's presence, shouted: 'Come here and see your father, you little bastard!' Charles thought this was a terrible insult, so he gave his son a very grand title indeed. Thus are great families born. In fact, Charles felt so guilty about having so many illegitimate sons that he made them all dukes and earls – the Earldoms of Richmond, Grafton and Lennox were all created in this way.

The 12th Duke of St Albans was a wonderful eccentric. He spent part of his final years travelling around America on a Greyhound bus, and caused a scandal when Queen Elizabeth II was crowned in 1953. Having discovered that he held the hereditary office of Master Falconer, the Duke told the organisers of the coronation that he would be attending the ceremony, as was his right, and he would also be carrying a live falcon. When the officials protested that this was absurd, the Duke pointed out that not only was he coming with a falcon, but it was his duty as laid down in statute to do so.

Panic ensued and a compromise was finally reached when the Duke agreed to attend the coronation with a bird –

but it would be stuffed rather than alive. So eccentric was the Duke – and so grand – that when not attending royal weddings he went several times a week to his club in St James's Street to find an underling who could wind his watch for him.

DRUGS FOR SALE

1955

If we take the historical view, it seems that the connection between crime and drugs is a relatively recent phenomenon. By making drugs illegal we made them very appealing to criminals who, of course, exploit addicts to the full in the knowledge that they will be able to get their drugs only from illegal sources and at very high prices.

It is common knowledge, for example, that poets like Coleridge and Tennyson took vast amounts of laudanum, as did Queen Victoria, and laudanum is simply a liquid form of opium. But what is less well known is that in London's chemists until the 1950s, most patent medicines for children and adults, whether for coughs and colds or more serious conditions, contained a pretty hefty shot of cocaine. The logic behind the inclusion of cocaine was simple: it made you feel better whatever happened to be wrong with you, and there was no evidence at that time that it was physiologically addictive.

The Oxford Street branch of Boots also sold a medicine known as Daffy's Elixir until around 1955. This was designed to soothe fractious children and contained opium. Even more extraordinary is the fact that, until the First World War, the most prestigious department store in London – Harrods in Knightsbridge – sold cocaine. And of course it was of the highest possible quality: 100 per cent pure!

LEGGING IT

1956

Over the centuries, many strange objects have been found in the River Thames. Poor children in the nineteenth and earlier centuries once patrolled the mudflats at low tide right across the capital looking for anything of value.

The prime scavenging area was the Port of London just below London Bridge, because it was here that ships from across the world crowded together and inevitably valuable items were lost overboard that could be retrieved when the tide was out. The 'mudlarks', as these children were known, worked barefoot and semi-naked in the mud right though the year, winter and summer, collecting copper nails, lumps of coal and occasionally things of greater value.

Modern mudlarks can still be seen with their metal detectors working the gravel banks at low tide, and over the years they have found many remarkable and sometimes highly valuable items, including gold crosses, medieval rings, Roman coins and even, on at least one occasion, a Bronze Age shield – the so-called 'Battersea Shield'.

But the prize for the strangest item ever found in the river must go to the contents of a wooden box found in 1956, just downstream from Lambeth Bridge. The carefully sealed wooden crate contained half a dozen beautifully made and hinged artificial legs and two sets of what looked like early Victorian surgical equipment. Both sets were first thought to be general doctor's tools, but in fact they were specialist tools designed to be used by surgeons whose main work involved amputating limbs.

In the nineteenth century, surgeons who removed limbs considered themselves an elite group and they vied with each other to see who could remove a limb in the shortest possible time. Speed was important because before the invention of anaesthetics the patient was given a great deal of alcohol to drink and then simply held down while the surgeon got to work, and a patient in agony could not be held still for long.

The box may have had some connection with St Thomas's Hospital, which is a short distance from Lambeth Bridge on the south side of the river, but this has never been proven to be the case.

LOLITA
IN LONDON
1959

One of the strangest tales from literary London concerns the
publication of Vladimir Nabokov's novel *Lolita* in 1959. The
manuscript came into the hands of the London publishers
Weidenfeld & Nicolson, then based in Bloomsbury. The
firm had been founded by George Weidenfeld, an Austrian
Jew who came to London to escape Nazi persecution, and
Nigel Nicolson, the Old Etonian son of the writer Vita
Sackville-West and her husband Harold Nicolson.

Weidenfeld & Nicolson feared they would be prosecuted
if they published Nabokov's book (it tells the story of a
middle-aged man's obsession with a pubescent girl) despite
strongly believing in its literary merits. So they came up
with a plan to tempt the Lord Chancellor (who was still
employed at that time to censor books) into prosecuting
them. Under the Obscene Publications Act, an offence was
committed only if a publication deemed to be obscene was
sold by a publisher to a member of the public. Without that
sale, no offence had been committed. So Nigel Nicolson,
who looked after editorial matters at the publisher, sold a
single copy to a woman in the office and then told the Lord
Chancellor what he had done and invited him to prosecute.

In his letter to the Lord Chancellor, Nicolson included a
deadline and said that if the firm hadn't been prosecuted by
that date, they would assume all was well and publish the
book. On the eve of the deadline, nothing had been heard,

so Weidenfeld & Nicolson organised a huge party, taking the whole of the ground floor of the Ritz to entertain friends and family – and, of course, authors. Halfway through the evening, they received a communication from the Lord Chancellor's office which read: 'We have decided it would not be in the public interest in this case to prosecute. Enjoy your party.'

Lolita sold more than 80,000 copies in the following three weeks and established Weidenfeld & Nicolson as a major British publisher.

HORSE WORSHIP
1960

St John's Hyde Park Crescent looks like any other Victorian English church, but it is very unusual in at least one respect: each year it organises an event known as Horseman's Sunday or the Blessing of the Horses. The event, which began around 1960, usually occurs in September, and the idea is to celebrate horse riding in London, for, despite the growth of London traffic and the loss of green spaces, riding still continues in the capital. St John's has an especially close connection with horses because it is very near Rotten Row in Hyde Park, where riding has taken place for over 400 years.

Hyde Park Stables still offers visitors the chance to ride a pony along the route that was once used by the royal family ('Rotten Row' is a corruption of *Route du Roi*, French for 'King's Row') to ride from St James's Palace to their residence in Kensington. In Victorian and Edwardian times it became a place to see and be seen on Sundays, when the great and the good would greet each other from their carriages or from the backs of their horses. And there was huge (unacknowledged) competition to have the best-presented horse and, for the riders, the finest coats, hats, whips and spurs.

On Horseman's Sunday, the vicar of St John's leads a cavalcade of horses to the church to celebrate this equine tradition, and the tradition states that the vicar must himself be mounted. So far no vicar is recorded as having ever fallen off!

CHURCH HOUSE

1963

One of the strangest examples of architecture in London can be found near the junction of Love Lane and Wood Street in the City. Here you will find St Alban Tower, which has been converted into flats. This is the only remaining part of the old Church of St Alban Wood Street. The medieval church that stood here was rebuilt in the 1630s by the great classical architect Inigo Jones, only to be destroyed in the Great Fire of 1666. Wren's replacement church was then destroyed in the Blitz, leaving the tower and the outer walls, which were demolished in 1963. The tower bizarrely became a private house and it still is – what's more, it is situated on a traffic island!

BILLY'S PALACE IN THE MALL

1965

William Tallon was one of the most extraordinary characters of the twentieth century. For over 50 years, from 1965, he was the most trusted servant of the late Queen Mother. The son of a shopkeeper from the Midlands, Tallon was in fact far more than a servant – the Queen Mother took him everywhere with her and their relationship caused huge problems in the royal household because HRH made it very clear that even her aristocratic advisers were of less value to her than Tallon. She once famously said to an adviser who disliked Billy, 'Your job is negotiable. Billy's is not.'

It was this attitude that led many people to think of Billy and the Queen Mother almost as one would think of a couple. He may have been a servant – his official title was Groom of the Backstairs – but most observers thought he was far more like the Queen Mother's life partner. They dressed up in fancy dress together, went out for private lunches, attended the opera together and partied late into the night. Tallon was a key element in the organisation of the Queen Mother's favourite daily event – lunch. He made her guests drinks and helped them relax so that they could entertain the Queen Mother. Most servants were given a small bedsitting room at the top of one or other of the royal London palaces, but, after a time, Tallon was given a little house of his own. This strange little house – which he called 'my little palace in the Mall' – became the scene of constant riotous parties where Tallon would entertain his many friends with champagne and endless jokes and anecdotes.

His only stipulation was that his guests should leave quietly as the Queen Mother – whose bedroom was just a few hundred feet away – slept with her bedroom window open. Tallon stayed in his 'little palace' until the Queen Mother's death in 2002. From the outside, the house is unchanged since Tallon's time – he died in 2007 – and it can still be seen, rather like a low-built Georgian bungalow, halfway along the Mall towards Admiralty Arch from Buckingham Palace.

SPIKY BRIDGE

1973

The current London Bridge is the third to cross the river at this point on the Thames, and it is also the least interesting. Gone are the towers and turrets of earlier structures; the picturesque houses and privies overhanging the water. But the bridge's most gruesome feature had always been the long wooden spikes that stood high above the towers built at the southern end. It was on these spikes that for centuries traitors' heads were impaled.

When the old bridge was demolished, the new Georgian bridge was built slightly upstream of the old bridge (in the process destroying the seventeenth-century Fishmongers' Hall) but all traces of those old barbarous spikes were removed.

When the Georgian bridge was sold in the 1960s and shipped stone by stone to the United States, in 1973 a new, purely functional bridge was built to replace it. This is the bridge we now have, but if you look at the southern end of the bridge you will see a large spike – is this a modern version of the ones from the bridge's gruesome past? In fact, the Southwark Gateway Needle – as it is called – built in 1999, is a marker that points to the place at which the medieval London Bridge crossed the river.

CAB RULES

1976

Until the 1950s it was still a requirement of London taxi drivers to keep a bag of hay somewhere in the cab. This may seem silly, but it was simply that the rules had not been changed since the last hansom cab had been licensed as recently as 1947.

Hansoms were horse-pulled cabs. Add this to the fact that the old cab drivers' shelters were still identical to the ones used at the end of the nineteenth century and it is easy to see why, in the world of the London cabby, things change slowly.

This may also explain why the black cab we see today has hardly changed at all since its introduction. Even in the 1960s the space next to the driver was still open to the elements – it was where luggage had to be tied in with leather straps because the boot (in theory) still contained that bale of hay. Some other very strange cab-driving traditions survived into the 1970s.

Until 1976, for example, all cabs had to be made so that the roof in the passengers' compartment was high enough to let an average-height man keep his top hat on. And, to this day, it is perfectly legal for a cab driver to get out of their cab anywhere in London and urinate in broad daylight – just so long as he goes to the offside back of the cab to do it!

CLUB RULES

1977

London clubs are one of the capital's more embarrassing features. Some refuse to have women members; most don't allow visitors. The very grand clubs – White's, Boodles and so on – don't even identify themselves by having a name plaque on the front door, presumably to avoid the risk of common people wandering in.

But the oldest clubs have performed at least one great service – they have preserved one or two splendid buildings that would almost certainly have been demolished without them. And a very curious tale surrounds the fate of one of the less fortunate of these clubs – the Junior Carlton.

The Junior Carlton was set up in response to the Second Reform Act of 1867, which created a whole new set of electors. It was called the Junior Carlton because prospective members – though Tory to a man – knew they had no hope of being admitted to the Carlton Club itself. They were not from old families and had only recently made their money, so they were not quite acceptable to the members of the older club. Membership of the Carlton proper was reserved for far grander figures of the establishment.

The Junior Carlton's clubhouse, a large and rather splendid nineteenth-century building, was at 30 Pall Mall. All went well until 1963, when the people who ran the club decided to sell their building in order to buy the land next to it. The land they had their eye on had formerly been occupied by the Carlton Club, but it had been destroyed by a bomb in the Second World War. The plan went ahead, and the committee that ran the Junior Carlton bought the plot and decided to build what they described as 'the club of the future': a box made of concrete, steel and glass. Within months of the new building opening, however, the members began to cancel their subscriptions in droves. In 1977 the Junior Carlton merged with the Carlton Club as virtually all its members had left.

CANAL MONEY

1978

Over the years, London's canals have gradually been
transformed from industrial highways designed to carry
coal and steel and other heavy goods to leisure and wildlife
corridors. Where once the old coal barges slowly passed
gasworks and factories as they crossed London, now those
same boats are filled with holidaymakers or Londoners
who have decided to live on the canal. But even in the dark
industrial days, the water in the canals was never as polluted
as the River Thames.

The canals may have looked dirty, but the lack of current
meant there was never any point in discharging sewage into
them as there wouldn't be anywhere for it to go. And so for
that reason London's canals have always been a haven for
wildfowl and, perhaps most surprising of all, fish.

Huge pike up to 3¼ft (1m) long certainly inhabit the
Grand Union and Regent's Park canals and are occasionally
caught by anglers, who tend to make their catches early
in the morning and are not usually seen by the tourists
ploughing up and down the canal in leisure boats. Among
the stranger catches reported by anglers are crayfish – a
sort of miniature freshwater lobster – Japanese spider
crabs, and even trout! But perhaps most peculiar of all was
the catch made by a young man fishing the Grand Union
Canal behind King's Cross Station in 1978.

He had caught several good roach and was thinking about going home when something made him try one more cast. Out went his line. Ten minutes later he reeled in and assumed he had snagged an old boot. Something heavy was attached to his line but it was clearly some rubbish rather than a live fish. The 'rubbish' turned out to be a plastic bag containing £5,000, far more than an average year's wages at the time!

MAD WILLIE
1980

If you are in Elm Park, Chelsea, and happen across a restaurant called The Henry Root, you might be forgiven for wondering who on earth Henry Root was. Well, Root was in fact the pseudonym of William Donaldson (1935–2005), one of London's most eccentric writers.

The son of a millionaire shipping magnate, Donaldson went from Winchester College to Cambridge and then joined the Royal Navy as part of his National Service, but he couldn't wait – as he often put it himself – to get involved in the real life of London.

That meant drugs, prostitutes and an extravagant lifestyle that saw him work his way through a vast inherited fortune in just a few years. Donaldson used the money he received upon the death of his father to boost the early careers of poets Ted Hughes and Sylvia Plath, among others. He also funded much of the theatrical boom of the 1960s. Most famously, he produced the hugely successful satire *Beyond the Fringe*, although he was later accused of taking almost all the profits from it while paying the stars of the show, including Alan Bennett and Jonathan Miller, a pittance.

An enormously generous man in other respects, Donaldson eventually ran out of money, partly because he insisted on promoting comedies that had no chance of success. Penniless, he became a pimp in a brothel for a number of years – an experience he recounted in his only published novel.

But it was his book *The Henry Root Letters*, first published in 1980, that made him famous and earned him another fortune, although by this time he was a crack cocaine addict, and much of his newfound wealth was to be spent on drugs.

The Henry Root Letters were a marvellous lampoon of the rich and famous. To create the book, Donaldson simply wrote to politicians, publishers, famous sports people, police constables and many other prominent people. He wrote absurd but apparently serious letters under the pseudonym Henry Root, and then published them together with the replies he received from his targets. The result was a masterpiece of satire. But drugs and heavy smoking took their toll and Donaldson died at the age of 70 in 2005.

HORSE HIGH

c.1990

Horses have never quite disappeared from London's streets. Until well into the 1950s, milk was delivered by horse and cart in less affluent parts of the city. And even in the 1970s, the totters, or rag-and-bone men, still used ponies to pull their carts through the streets, and the cry 'Any old iron' was, if you like, an early plea for recycling. The totters also made a good living collecting scrap metal, and their income was boosted at least in part because they had no fuel bills to pay. This benefit was especially apparent when petrol prices began to soar in the early 1970s.

The totters and milk vans had gone by the 1990s, but one group of horses still had a decade and more to add their splendour to the streets, as at least two of London's oldest brewers retained their massive beer drays and the shire horses that pulled them. They did this partly because horses and colourful carts were a good advertisement for their beer, but also because delivering in this way to local pubs owned by breweries, such as Young's in Wandsworth and Fuller's in Chiswick, made economic sense. Young's and Fuller's finally gave up on their horses in the early years of this century, but horses can still be seen in the form of police horses, a common sight on the streets of central London, and their existence explains a feature of the city that baffles Londoners and visitors alike. Traffic lights across the capital, as elsewhere, always have a separate post to which the lights that tell pedestrians it is safe to cross are fixed.

The button that pedestrians press is sensibly about a metre from the ground, but where horses still cross a duplicate button exists around 7ft (2.1m) from the ground; these are known as Pegasus crossings. Visitors sometimes notice these buttons and joke that some Londoners must be giants, but the devices exist simply to allow police riders to stop the traffic without the need to dismount and press the lower button. No one seems quite sure when they were installed, but they were probably first fitted during the 1990s.

SEX AT THE
BRITISH MUSEUM

1999

The British establishment has always had a strange attitude to the ancient world. For centuries – certainly more than half a millennium – the British education system was entirely dominated by the study of Latin and Greek.

Generations of schoolboys ploughed laboriously through ancient texts, while books written in English and other modern languages were entirely neglected. For centuries the only English texts studied at Oxford were Chaucer and Shakespeare. The dominance of classical languages seems odd when one remembers that those most assiduously promoting their study were clergymen – both Oxford and Cambridge existed until recently to train men destined for ordination in the church, yet it seems only rarely to have occurred to them that the texts they spent so long studying were written by people who were pagans – pagans, moreover, who had already been in hell for a very long time.

It was equally obvious to many of course that the authors of the ancient Greek and Latin texts could not have been Christian even if they'd wanted to, because Christianity did not exist at the time they lived. This meant that elaborate adjustments had to be made to the design of hell to accommodate those who could not go to heaven because they were pagans, but could hardly be consigned to hell for not believing something they had never heard of.

One of the greatest difficulties with ancient texts, and even more so with ancient art, was that it was often obscene, especially in the eyes of nineteenth-century Britain – no matter that ancient sculptures were also seen as the highest achievement of art. Something had to be done to protect not just the innocent, but pretty much everyone from ancient sensuality. This meant that youngsters were permitted to study, for example, Catullus, who wrote about men having sex with boys, but risqué statues and pottery decorated with 'obscene' pictures had to be hidden.

And this is how the British Museum Secretum, one of London's strangest institutions, came into being. The Secretum (or 'secret museum') was a closed store where all the beautiful but immoral art was kept. In Victorian times it was packed with statues and pottery as it was felt that young Victorian ladies simply could not be exposed to what today would seem the most innocent examples of nude art.

The thinking behind this prudery was never clear. When pressed, officials would suggest vaguely that women were both easily shocked (being so delicate) and very easily corrupted. Some thought when women fainted they never fully recovered; others felt they might instantly become lascivious prostitutes.

Entry to the Secretum was not entirely forbidden even in the most prudish period of the nineteenth century, however. 'Mature gentlemen' could apply for a special ticket, but numbers were limited. In the first years after the Secretum was officially sanctioned in 1865, only 2,000–3,000 people each year managed to get a ticket, but word soon got around and the museum authorities were outraged as the number of applications dramatically increased.

Among the artefacts hidden away for decades was the famous statue of the Tara, a gilt bronze, three-quarter life-size female bodhisattva – a Buddhist figure. Today it is almost impossible to understand what the fuss was all about as the Tara is simply a curvaceous female figure with large breasts. Apparently breasts were a tremendous problem for our Victorian predecessors. Astonishingly, the vast quantity of racy material in the Secretum was still there, hidden away, until as recently as the mid-1960s. It was gradually removed and added to the normal collections in the museum's various rooms and, you will be relieved to hear, there were no reports of ladies fainting or suddenly turning to a life of prostitution. One or two items are still kept in the Secretum today. (If you'd like to see them simply ask to see the contents of cupboards 54 and 55!)

Controversy still rages about some museum artefacts – a recent case concerns the Warren Cup. This magnificent silver cup, made around the fifth century AD, is decorated with several scenes of men having sex with boys. When the museum bought the cup in 1999 for the enormous sum of just under £2 million there was an outcry and, despite the extraordinary quality of the cup, there were many who thought it should be melted down rather than displayed in a museum. It then emerged that the cup had been offered to the British Museum for far less than they eventually had to pay for it, but during the 1960s. It was turned down because, at that time, the Archbishop of Canterbury was a trustee of the museum. However, the cup survived and is not currently in the Secretum!

LOST AND FOUND

2000

One of the greatest and least known London institutions is the London Transport lost property office. Over the century and more that it has existed it has found itself in receipt of some extraordinary items that have been lost or abandoned on the Underground network. Thousands of sets of false teeth, for example, as well as numerous wooden legs, wigs, shotguns, grenades, a set of surgical instruments, a human skeleton in a box, a seventeenth-century landscape painting and even a suit of armour.

Other oddities include a full-size jukebox, several record players, trumpets, a cello and on one occasion even a double bass. A pram was discovered in the 1950s full of empty gin bottles, and just after the Second World War a first edition of the 1563 *Actes and Monuments* (popularly known as *Foxe's Book of Martyrs*) – worth around £10,000 today – was discovered on a seat on the District Line.

Dogs and cats are frequently found, along with more unusual pets including several parrots, snakes, a toucan and even a baby alligator. But prizes for the strangest things ever to be found on the London Underground should probably go to the following items: breast implants, a wedding dress, a First World War gas mask, a stuffed piranha fish, a lollipop lady's lollipop and, in 2000, a 5ft (1.5m) high teddy bear with an Albanian address label on it.

WILD UNDERGROUND

2005

The London Underground, famously the oldest subterranean railway in the world, is extraordinary for so many reasons that it is hard to know where to begin.

Many people think that it is so solid and ancient that it requires little maintenance. In fact, the opposite is true – when the trains stop running at night an army of cleaners, repair workers, electricians, track experts, bricklayers and stonemasons descend into the tunnels to check that all is well.

Each day a staggering 6 million gallons (30 million litres) of water has to be pumped out of the system – the problem is that the water table gets higher in London every year and will soon have to be kept out of the basements of houses and offices.

In the century and more since the Underground opened, dozens of babies have been born on the lines – the District Line apparently holds the record for the highest number of births. Several murders have been committed on the Underground and on several occasions Underground trains have been used in funeral processions. Most famously, Thomas Barnardo – of Barnardo children's homes fame – was carried to his final resting place on the Tube.

But in recent years the Underground has become something far more extraordinary – it is now one of the most important sites in London for wildlife. People forget that much of the system is not underground at all – many of the lines run for miles out beyond the tunnels into the suburbs, and it is here that these wildlife corridors, as they are known, help both rare and common species survive and thrive. Among the creatures recorded are sparrowhawks, owls, deer, foxes, voles and even the rare great-crested newt. In 2005, kestrels and a red kite were spotted.

And though much of the network has been modernised, traces of the earliest days of the Underground do remain – Baker Street Station, beloved of Sherlock Holmes fans, has been restored to its Victorian splendour by reopening the brick lighting tunnels above the platforms, and at Greenford Station you can still see the last of the wooden escalators.

While you are travelling about on the Underground, keep a careful eye on the buskers who now perform perfectly legally at many central London stations. Many famous singers began their careers as buskers, including Rod Stewart and Ed Sheeran, and occasionally you might spot a celebrity who has decided a bit of busking might be fun (especially if they have a film crew in tow). Recent sightings have included Paul McCartney in Covent Garden in 2013 and Nile Rodgers on the South Bank in 2015.

NOT A BROTHEL

2010

Meard Street in Soho, mostly pedestrianised, narrow and easily overlooked, is one of London's most interesting thoroughfares. It runs east to west from Dean Street to Wardour Street and includes a short run of early eighteenth-century houses, each with their interiors largely intact.

Meard Street was formerly two courts blocked off from one another at the halfway point of the present street, and for a number of years it was home to one of London's greatest modern eccentrics, Sebastian Horsley (1962–2010). An artist and writer, Horsley once had himself crucified to find out what it felt like. He also claimed that he only liked to have sex with prostitutes and, indeed, had worked himself as a prostitute for a number of years. He also insisted that legalising prostitution would spoil all the fun.

As Soho became more respectable, he lamented the change and the final straw came when one of his favourite haunts, the Colony Room, finally closed. He said of Soho: 'The air used to be clean and the sex used to be dirty. Now it is the other way around.' He became famous not just for his lifestyle but also for his paintings of crosses and for his outrageous comments, which were always reported in the newspapers.

He was found dead following a drug overdose in 2010. More than 400 mourners attended his funeral at St James's Church, Piccadilly, for, despite his strange lifestyle and drug taking, he was a charming and friendly man. Nonetheless, many were astonished at the number of people he knew, who were from all walks of life. Horsley's lasting monument and final marvellous joke can be found at his old house, No. 7 Meard Street. The sign he put on the door remains and has become part of Soho legend; it reads in large white capital letters, 'This is not a brothel. There are no prostitutes at this address.'

FATBERG TOUR

2013

The Abbey Mills pumping station near West Ham Station and Lee Valley Park is a magnificent, half Italian Renaissance, half gothic monument to one of the greatest engineers Britain has ever produced. Joseph Bazalgette (1819–91) created the sewage system on which London still relies.

At a time when millions of tons of untreated sewage entered the River Thames each year, he designed and helped to build an extraordinary network of gigantic sewers that carry most of London's waste to Beckton, a huge sewage treatment centre in east London where it is all cleaned and then released into the Thames Estuary. But what makes Abbey Mills really unusual is that you can apply for a tour of the building, which includes a visit to the sewers themselves. Bazalgette himself appears to have walked almost every yard of his new sewer system, and even today the 6ft (1.8m) diameter tunnels are a marvel of intricate brickwork, for these sewers had to be built without the benefits of concrete, which was yet to be invented.

Cleverly, Bazalgette designed his system in such a way that raw sewage was always diluted by rainwater runoff and bathwater, so the experience of walking the tunnels is not as dreadful as you might imagine. Bazalgette was also an extraordinary visionary. He calculated the maximum amount of sewage he thought each Londoner would produce each year and used that to calculate the diameter of his sewer tunnels. Then, to allow for future population growth, he decided to double all his calculations – the result was a system that has lasted largely unaltered to this day. But some things about the sewer system might well have surprised even Bazalgette.

Wonderfully efficient though they are, the sewers regularly produce something that might have been invented by science fiction writers: not giant rats (rodents are in fact virtually unheard of in the system as the water levels are too high), nor dead bodies, but 'fatbergs'. Created by an accumulation of cooking fat from human waste they can become as big as a double-decker bus – in fact, a fatberg discovered in the sewers under Leicester Square was equivalent to six double-decker buses. Another found at Kingston in 2013 weighed 15 tons. So if you take the tour – beware!